# IN DEFENSE
# OF NATO

# IN DEFENSE
# OF NATO

## The Alliance's Enduring Value

Keith A. Dunn

**Westview Press**
BOULDER, SAN FRANCISCO, & LONDON

In Memory of
William O. Staudenmaier
1931–1988

This Westview softcover edition is printed on acid-free paper and bound in library-quality, coated covers that carry the highest rating of the National Association of State Textbook Administrators, in consultation with the Association of American Publishers and the Book Manufacturers' Institute.

Published in 1990 in the United States of America by Westview Press, Inc., 5500 Central Avenue, Boulder, Colorado 80301, and in the United Kingdom by Westview Press, 13 Brunswick Centre, London WC1N 1AF, England

Library of Congress Cataloging-in-Publication Data
Dunn, Keith A.
  In defense of NATO : the Alliance's enduring value / Keith A.
  Dunn.
  p.    cm.
  Includes bibliographical references.
  ISBN 0-8133-0975-1
  1. North Atlantic Treaty Organization.  2. Europe—Defenses.
3. United States—Military relations—Europe.  4. Europe—Military
relations—United States.  I. Title.
UA646.3.D84  1990
355'.031'091821—dc20                                                89-27613
                                                                         CIP

Printed and bound in the United States of America

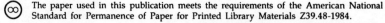 The paper used in this publication meets the requirements of the American National Standard for Permanence of Paper for Printed Library Materials Z39.48-1984.

10    9    8    7    6    5    4    3    2    1

# Contents

Arms Control, 72
Force Structure, 74
Conclusion, 76

# Tables and Figures

# Acknowledgments

I have never been impressed with acknowledgments that saved the most important people for last. Therefore, I express my appreciation first to those who had to make the greatest sacrifices and without whose understanding this book would not have been possible: my family— Terry, Chrisie, and Drew. Each of them had to give up something so I could have not only the time but also the peace and quiet necessary to write. I am grateful for their understanding that baseball, assistance with homework, and family chores sometimes had to take a backseat to Dad's time on the computer.

Also, I thank my colleagues in the Institute for National Strategic Studies and the Strategic Concepts Development Center. Several of them, particularly Stephen Flanagan, Karl Lowe, Bill Hogan, Andrew Hamilton, and Jeff Simon, read more drafts of chapters than I care to remember and they care to think about. Stephen Flanagan suffered probably the most because his office adjoined mine. I am sure that the words "what do you think of this?" send cold chills down his spine because as soon as I would utter those fateful words I would rush into his office, interrupt whatever he was doing, and try my latest idea or chapter transition on him. The only way that he could escape me was to take a new job with the Policy Planning Staff at the Department of State. Andrew Hamilton also deserves a special note of thanks. He tried, most unsuccessfully I must add, to teach me how to perform mathematical formulas on his "fancy" Hewlett-Packard calculator. Thank goodness he was willing to check my old-fashioned pencil-and-paper techniques and then recalculate them when that proved necessary.

This book is dedicated to William O. Staudenmaier, a good friend, an excellent strategist, and the rarest of all commodities—a first-rate uniformed scholar. His premature death was a loss to all who knew him. I think that he would have liked the approach used in this book, if not its ultimate conclusion. I hope that is the case.

Nothing in this volume should be construed to represent the official position of the National Defense University, the Department of the Army, or the Department of Defense, unless so designated by other official documentation. I alone am responsible for any errors of fact or judgment.

*Keith A. Dunn*
Washington, D.C.

# 1

# The NATO Consensus Under Attack

This book is about the strategic importance of NATO-Europe and why, for the foreseeable future, Western Europe should continue to remain the primary geographic area of importance in U.S. national security planning. In many ways, it is a shame that a book like this has to be written, given the enduring importance of Western Europe in U.S. global planning in the twentieth century. Nevertheless, NATO bashing—it seems—has become a popular American pastime. Over the last several years, several influential Americans—Zbigniew Brzezinski, Henry Kissinger, Congresswoman Patricia Schroeder, former Senator Gary Hart, and Andrew Goodpaster, to name just a few—have advocated or implied that the United States unilaterally should withdraw large portions of its forces from Europe. Additionally, there seems to have been a ground swell of support within the academic community favoring an alteration in the U.S. relationship with Western Europe.

While there has been a lot of publicity given to such proposals, insufficient attention to the strategic merits or wisdom of such suggestions has occurred. Consequently, there are significant issues concerning the importance of NATO to U.S. strategy, Europe's current contribution to its own defense, and the long range consequences of a potential major withdrawal of U.S. forces from Europe that have not been adequately addressed. Before policymakers and congressional leaders can evaluate the merits of the choices before them, a comprehensive review of the national security implications associated with changing the American security relationship with Europe is necessary.

Any hope that a debate about the importance of Europe to the United States will be transitory is unlikely. If anything, this debate will probably intensify over the next several years for at least two reasons. First, much like the continental-maritime strategy debate that filled the pages of newspapers and academic journals during the early years of the Reagan Administration, the issue of whether we should or should not retain a substantial number of U.S. forces in Europe for the foreseeable future is a fundamental debate about the strategic challenges facing the United States: namely, how does the United States secure its vital objectives in Europe, the Far East, and the Persian Gulf—while dealing with more likely conflicts in the Third World—without needlessly increasing the risk of war in areas where deterrence failure could mean nuclear war? And, equally important, how can the United States afford such a strategy, when its defense budget growth is unlikely to do better than keep even with inflation over the next several years.

Second, the whole issue of alliance burdensharing has become a significant American political issue. In an era of tighter defense budgets, the issue of forward deployment of U.S. forces—with NATO-Europe begin the lightning rod, since more than 350,000 U.S. forces are deployed in this region—has become a politically debatable topic. One would hope that debates concerning national security interests and objectives would be above partisan domestic politics. But, in a democracy such as exists within the United States, only the politically naive would believe such an argument. National security and defense issues affect domestic political decisions and vice versa. Therefore, it is difficult, if not impossible, to divorce a fundamental debate about national security interests and objectives from partisan politics in a democracy. The best that one can hope for is that the right questions are asked and that the advocates of change are forced to demonstrate that their alternatives *clearly* would result in a more secure international environment. This book argues that making fundamental changes in the U.S. security commitment to Europe would not be in the United States' long term interests. But, what about the basic questions that need to be asked?

The fundamental strategic questions fall within six major categories: (1) Why does the United States forward deploy military forces in Europe: are they there for altruistic purposes or reasons of U.S. national security? (2) Is the concept of U.S. forward defense anchored in Western Europe and the Far East still necessary? Could the U.S. "go it alone" without allies in a U.S.-Soviet crisis? (3) Have the conditions or reasons for a substantial U.S. presence in Western Europe substantially changed: i.e., has the threat changed in such a demonstrative manner that the United States should rethink its traditional geographic force deployment patterns? (4) If the United States could withdraw forces from Europe, would that be desirable? (5) What are the political and military costs and risks— not only in Western Europe, but also outside of NATO—that could be associated with withdrawing a major portion of U.S. forces from Europe? (6) Would the United States be better off with a smaller presence in Europe, or is the status quo better than the possible alternatives that could emerge?

Subsequent chapters will address each of these issues in detail. However, before doing this, we need to set the strategic stage by very briefly discussing the important schools of thought that favor fundamental changes in the American commitment to NATO, some red-herrings that complicate analysis, some of the causes for the breakdown in the consensus in support of NATO, and reasons why the current debate seems to be different from earlier ones that have occurred during NATO's history.

## Schools of Thought

Throughout this book I will refer to critics of NATO. The plural is used intentionally, because, in many respects, there is no single identifiable school of thought or list of objective criteria that "NATO's critics" can agree upon. Rather, there is a disparate group of critics—from all ends of the political spectrum—who at times end up advocating the same end result but for different reasons. As a result, those who favor making major—sometimes radical—changes in the American-European security relationship sometimes can disagree among themselves as strongly as they do with supporters of the status quo.

Despite disagreements, however, there are some common threads that run through the various arguments favoring major changes in the trans-Atlantic partnership. They are:

- Europe is not as strategically important to the United States as it once was. Other areas of the world are economically, politically, and culturally increasing in importance. As a result, U.S. force deployments and regional priorities need to be adjusted to reflect these new geostrategic realities. Observers who see a shift in the world's economic center of gravity from Western Europe to the Pacific often make this argument. Frequently, advocates of a U.S. maritime strategy argue that the Pacific Ocean region should be elevated, at least to an equal status with Europe, in the Department of Defense's (DoD) planning process. Naval spokesmen often have used economic indicators to bolster their case. However, more often than not, this is a force structure or service budget argument rather than a strategic issue for the Navy. Elevating the status of the Pacific, or lowering the importance of Europe, in DoD's planning process would justify more dollars spent on the Navy rather than the Army or Air Force during the DoD budget review process, since the Pacific is predominantly a naval theater of action.
- NATO-Europe has historically refused to pay its fair share of the burden to defend itself. There is the belief that the United States is paying a disproportionate share of NATO's defense burden; i.e.,

NATO-Europe is able, *but unwilling,* to bear the economic, political, and military costs to create a viable conventional defense. Some believe that if the United States would withdraw some forces from Western Europe, NATO nations would be forced to accept more responsibility for their own defense.

- Given the large U.S. deficits and trade imbalances, which some analysts believe are caused by the large defense budgets of the 1980s, the nation has few realistic options left. Financial realities will require a decline in DoD's budget over the next few years. Since NATO and NATO-related commitments comprise a large portion of the DoD budget (as much as 60 percent of DoD's budget, according to some calculations), critics argue that NATO should not be exempt from the budget knife. And, in fact, if managed properly, some analysts believe that the United States could benefit both financially and strategically. For example, David Calleo has argued that "East European defense is an area where enormous American budgetary savings might be made without diminishing either U.S. or European security."[1] By scaling back on the American unilateral guarantee to help Europeans defend themselves, Calleo and others argue that ultimately a more stable and enduring military situation can be created in Europe—i.e., Europeanization of Europe's defense.
- Major U.S. troop withdrawals from Europe, some critics argue, would result in significant defense budget savings—if true, not an unimportant goal in a period of tighter defense dollars—and would allow the United States to restructure forces for more likely contingencies in the Third World and other regions outside of Europe (e.g., Southwest Asia).

This book contends that each of these arguments is flawed. They are based on assertions, which in some cases are not accurate, or they require questionable facilitating assumptions to come true before they can appear to be appealing or practical. The basic arguments that will be made in subsequent chapters are:

- On the basis of some narrow indicators—trade for example—NATO may be relatively less important to the United States than it was 30 years ago. However, a more complete examination of economic, geopolitical, and sociological factors indicates that there is no reason now—or for the foreseeable future—why NATO-Europe should be displaced as the highest priority overseas region in U.S. National security planning or strategy.
- Generally, European efforts in support of NATO have not received a fair shake from many defense analysts. Unlike the American "boom-bust" approach to defense spending, Europeans seemed to have committed themselves to a slow, but steady growth pattern

over the last 15 years for which they have not been given credit. Additionally, NATO-Europe has not received sufficient recognition for the non-quantifiable ways that it has contributed to European defense. For example, European states provide the territory on which a war may be fought; they provide rent free access to bases and facilities for U.S. and other allied forces; and, the geographic location of NATO-European states complicates Soviet planning horizons. A Soviet military planner cannot be confident that military actions initiated by the USSR outside the NATO context subsequently might not spill back into the European area. Finally, traditional burden-sharing arguments based solely or primarily on percentages of Gross National Product (GNP) or Gross Domestic Product (GDP)—so called "hard data"—can be very misleading. Depending on what one chooses or does not choose to include in these types of economic calculations determines how well some NATO nations fare in the burdensharing debate. This issue will be discussed in more depth in Chapter 3.

- Granted, to argue that the extent of Western Europe's contribution to its own defense is not adequately appreciated is not the same as saying that the United States is or should be completely happy with the current state of NATO's military affairs. However, the sort of modifications and improvements that NATO most needs to adopt over the next 10–15 years—e.g., greater arms cooperation; improved sustainability; greater rationalization, standardization, and inter-operability among NATO forces; expanded protection for tactical aircraft while on the ground; better harmonization in the area of military doctrine; new planning initiatives; greater role specialization, etc.—will be encouraged or fostered only through effective Alliance management and accommodation by all parties, *not* by U.S. unilateral coercion or threats to bring some U.S. forces home if Europeans fail to accept an American definition of burdensharing.

- Pulling substantial forces out of Europe will neither save money, nor necessarily result in excess forces that could be reconfigured for lesser contingencies. Moreover, if the United States decided to withdraw major elements of its forces from Western Europe prior to a conventional arms control agreement that significantly reduced the Warsaw Pact threat, the United States would increase its level of risk in an area where the majority of Soviet forces will continue to be deployed, even if the USSR carries out Gorbachev's December 1988 offer to reduce Soviet forces in Eastern Europe.[2]

- It is not obvious that a more stable or secure European environment would develop from either a reduced U.S. presence in Europe or diminution in the American role within NATO's politico-military decisionmaking process. In fact, too much Europeanization of Europe's defense could trigger reactions detrimental to Western security. The United States should insist that Europeans can and must do more to strengthen the European portion of NATO's defense pillar. This makes not only good strategic sense but also is a political necessity for any American administration in its dealings with Congress. However, more radical solutions such as devolution of U.S. responsibility over the control of nuclear weapons and nuclear strategy, which is implicit in any call for a European military officer to become the Supreme Allied Commander in Europe (SACEUR), are premature.

• U.S. withdrawals from Europe while NATO is transitioning to a post-INF "zero-zero" environment, before European conventional arms reduction talks are completed, and while the U.S. and USSR are considering an arms control agreement that could reduce strategic nuclear forces by as much as 50 percent would be bad politics as well as bad strategy.

### Seductive Non-Issues

One reason why current critics of NATO often seem to gain the upper hand in the public debate is the manner in which basic questions are asked. Rather than concentrating on fundamental geopolitical and strategic issues, recent critics have often attempted to focus the debate on enticing, but distracting, non-issues.

What do I mean by distracting non-issues? Critics of the current U.S. strategy argue that the United States has other interests than Europe, that the current military situation in Europe would be more favorable to the West if Europeans would spend more on defense, that demands on U.S. forces outside of Europe are growing, and that obtaining money for future U.S. defense initiatives will be difficult. To a point the critics are right. Such statements, however, are not very helpful to a decision-maker who must decide whether or not the United States should fundamentally alter the policy and strategy that has guided U.S. national security planning since the end of World War II. Competing interests and objectives and the current strain on defense budgets are important issues. They must be confronted. How the United States deals with them, however, should be determined by an evaluation of its interests, objectives, and threats in various regions, as well as a better understanding of how American global interests and objectives are *interdependent*.

In other words, a region that is extremely important, but faces less of a military threat, may require fewer forward deployed U.S. forces than another region that is equally important but confronts an immediate, as well as clear and present, military threat. This does not mean that the first region is any less important to the United States than the second. It simply suggests that there are several instruments of power to demonstrate American interest in and commitment to particular regions of the world; how American decisionmakers use these instruments is the result of a complex interplay between interests, objectives, and threats.

Let's look at some of the more seductive sorts of questions that are often posed to raise doubts about continuing the U.S. presence in Europe as a way to demonstrate that it is possible to have concerns about the way NATO and West Europeans do their business, without coming to the conclusion that changing America's security guarantee to Europe is the only logical answer. *First*, should we be content with NATO's current state of military affairs? Of course not. Clearly most defense analysts would prefer that the ratio of tanks, artillery pieces, divisions, air wings, etc. were more favorable to NATO's security interests than they currently are. Likewise, most American defense specialists would like to see Europeans spend more on their own defense and obtain greater economies of scale within NATO through better role specialization and less duplication of military and procurement efforts.

However, we should not overlook the fact that our West European allies have been willing to invest scarce resources in defense in a steady way for the last 15–20 years. We may have preferred that they would have spent more. But, this desire should not cloud the fact that the Warsaw Pact's efforts over 40 years to build forces, maintain a military edge in Western Europe and manipulate European public opinions have not politically intimidated NATO into inaction.

Prudent American defense planners will never feel completely comfortable with the current situation, nor should they. With interior lines of communication, geographic proximity to Western Europe, and a more closed political system that poses fewer impediments to mobilization decisionmaking in a crisis, the USSR will always have certain geostrategic advantages over a reinforcing power like the United States. But, NATO is a defensive alliance. As a result, it does not have to match the Warsaw Pact gun for gun, airplane for airplane, or tank for tank. NATO must maintain a sufficiently robust posture so that Moscow cannot be confident that it can obtain its political objectives through the use of force. This condition seems to exist today, due in no small measure to our European allies' willingness to invest in their own future.

If one of the Soviet objectives in Europe is to fragment the alliance politically, NATO's critics may play into Soviet hands when they openly criticize NATO for not doing enough for itself and threatening to withdraw American forces. Rather than emphasizing the negative, U.S. strategy and policy should focus on the positive contributions that NATO has made for its own defense. At the same time, however, the U.S. should quietly, *but firmly*, push its Alliance partners to develop primarily European based initiatives. These initiatives should result in each NATO member increasing its contributions to the common defense in ways that are affordable and lead to a more favorable ratio of European and U.S. defense expenditures. This is the best way to build and maintain the necessary public consensus within Western Europe for NATO, as the World War II generation passes from the political scene.[3]

*Second*, would we like to see NATO do things differently? Of course we would. To argue—as I will in Chapter 4—that NATO has not always received a fair shake when some analysts add up its contributions to its own defense is not the same as saying one is totally happy with NATO's current state of military affairs. For example, NATO nations have been slow to buy sustainability, partly out of fear that too many war reserve stocks might make longer conventional war a more attractive option for the United States and lead to nuclear decoupling. While NATO may have made significant progress over the last 15 years in modernizing its forces, it has not done enough to provide adequate numbers of shelters to protect its aircraft on the ground. Many Americans would prefer to see West European nations field more reserve units that could be rapidly mobilized in crisis. Currently, NATO's operational reserve forces come primarily from American reinforcing units. The problem is that these forces might not arrive in time. But more importantly, with conscription—even given future West German demographic constraints—some NATO nations should have sufficiently trained manpower to form more reserve units rather than having a large unassigned manpower pool, as currently exists.[4] With more West European reserve units, NATO could well be on its way to creating an initial defense that was capable of defending NATO territory until American reinforcements arrived, especially if France is considered in the equation, even though formally it is not part of NATO's integrated military command structure.

If the United States wants to encourage West Europeans to address these sorts of issues over the next 10–15 years, it might have to change its approach. It is a fact of life that the force modernization efforts initiated by most NATO nations in the late 1960s and 1970s have now run their course or will be completed by the early 1990s. The primary goal for the future is to fill in the gaps and make the forces more efficient: sustainability, new operational concepts, increased readiness, more reserves, improved planning initiatives, etc. It is hard to imagine how lowering the American presence in Western Europe, without a major reduction in Warsaw Pact presence via arms control, would encourage NATO nations to deal with these issues. And, a partially successful conventional arms control regime could even be counter-productive, encouraging Europeans and Americans alike to believe that the "military threat" to Western Europe had been reduced when in reality it had not.

An unpleasant message that NATO leaders ultimately will have to communicate to each of their domestic constituencies is that arms control will not and cannot eliminate the need for continued prudent investments in defense. This is not the type of message that many European or American parliamentarians or electorates want to hear in the current era. But, it is a conclusion supported by geostrategic realities.

Those realities are that even if the USSR unilaterally demobilized massive numbers of its forces, it would still be the major military power on the Eurasian continent and the United States would have an interest in balancing that power. As a continental power the Soviet Union has interior lines of communication that are more secure than those of the United States. Unless the USSR undergoes dramatic, even historic, changes in its political system, as a relatively closed authoritarian state, it has fewer impediments to mobilizing forces in a crisis than either the United States or West European democracies. Also, it is closer to Western Europe than is the United States. While fewer Soviet forces in Eastern Europe might reduce the Warsaw Pact's short warning attack capabilities— a capability that has been exaggerated in any case in recent years—it may have little impact on overall Soviet operational capabilities. A major restructuring of Soviet forces in its Western military districts along the lines of the Corps/brigade model—tested at Minsk and in Hungary— could result in a better overall Soviet operational capability to execute its doctrine of maneuver warfare in the event deterrence fails.

The North Atlantic Assembly captured the essence of these geostrategic realities in its *NATO in the 1990's* report:

> A satisfactory East-West relationship cannot be taken for granted; it remains a goal to be pursued in Western policies, not yet an accomplished fact.
>
> It is particularly important that defence and arms control policies be effectively harmonized and seen as means toward the end of enhanced security, and not as ends in themselves. Neither arms build-ups nor force reductions necessarily guarantee more security. In the 1990s the Allies should not make the mistake of over-emphasizing one aspect to the detriment of the other. NATO will have to ensure that its defence policies do not undermine security by stimulating responses by the East that only perpetuate the arms race. On the other hand, the Allies must ensure that they are not so anxious for improved East-West relations that they neglect fundamental defence requirements.[5]

*Third,* will NATO's role and importance in U.S. strategy change? Of course it will; if it does not, we should be concerned because, as in life, something which is static tends to atrophy and die. Some economic and demographic trends suggest that Western Europe may become less significant to the United States. However, as Chapter 3 will indicate, we are talking about trends over the next 40 to 50 years, not tomorrow or even the year 2000.

For the foreseeable future, Western Europe will continue to be the prize in U.S.-Soviet superpower competition. It will also be an important fulcrum in U.S.-Soviet competition in the Middle East, North Africa, and Southwest Asia. We should avoid tactical and operational options that could not only raise the level of risk in Europe but also create a self-fulfilling prophecy. It is clear that Moscow continues to believe that Western Europe is the global strategic center of gravity and is its primary strategic focus. That is why the Soviet Union will more than likely continue to deploy the majority of its forces against Western Europe and the Warsaw Pact will retain a numerical superiority over NATO's forces, even if the USSR carries out Gorbachev's December 1988 pledge to reduce Soviet military presence in Europe.

Politically and militarily, Western Europe has been more stable in the last 40 years than possibly at any time in its history. NATO, supported by the American nuclear guarantee and commitment to forward defense, has played some role in this—even if one cannot quantify the exact product. Furthermore, we have had significant political influence in European affairs over the years because of our large standing and ready military force deployed in and around the region. This presence, and the possibility that we might bring some U.S. forces home if we ever became too unhappy with the course of European events, has allowed us to have some impact on the course of European decisions—not just the military, but also political and economic decisions. A reduction of U.S. presence in Western Europe that occurred outside of a conventional arms control agreement would undermine that political leverage because the threat of doing something is often more effective than the actual decision.

*Finally,* should we send the bulk of the U.S. force structure to the Central Region if war should occur? Maybe not. But that is a question which should be decided only if and when deterrence fails and should be based on how much warning we have, how the battle or battles are going, and the nature and scope of conflict in other regions. Without a negotiated and verifiable conventional arms control agreement that significantly reduces the Warsaw Pact threat and increases the amount of "actionable" warning time for NATO in a major way, the equivalents of five American divisions and nine tactical fighter wings stationed in

Europe seem a relatively small price to pay for deterrence, particularly when one thinks about the costs in manpower and blood that would be spent should deterrence fail.[6]

## Current Malaise

The United States unilateral guarantee to help West Europeans defend themselves has been one of the most fundamental principles of U.S. national security policy in the post World War II period. Knowledgeable observers will obviously note that U.S.-NATO relations have never been completely harmonious. Differences concerning threat perceptions, burdensharing, out-of-area problems, nuclear issues, the search for an independent West European identity and solution to indigenous European problems, and German reunification have caused Alliance tensions on a variety of occasions.

Over the years, the United States has reacted militarily to numerous crises outside of Western Europe and, in some cases, became involved in prolonged conflicts (e.g., Korea and Vietnam) that adversely affected our abilities to defend Western Europe had a crisis arisen there. Nevertheless, from at least the end of World War II until the early 1980s, the predominant consensus within Washington's national security decision-making community—regardless of the political party in power—was that a secure Western Europe was one of the cornerstones of U.S. foreign and defense policy.

That consensus is now questioned. It is questioned to such a degree that serious strategic thinkers like Brzezinski and Kissinger have recommended that the United States unilaterally withdraw up to 100,000 U.S. forces from Europe in an effort to enhance American capabilities to react to the multitude of current and future worldwide threats that they envision. In later chapters, we will go into more detail why various advocates believe that the United States should unilaterally withdraw forces from Europe. Suffice it to say for the time being, the post-World War II consensus about Western Europe's primacy seems to have begun breaking down around 1980.

The reasons why the consensus is being attacked are interconnected and multifaceted, but three events, it seems, were most important. First, the Shah of Iran was deposed in 1979. This ultimately undermined the fundamentals of U.S. strategy for the entire Southwest Asian region. Then, Iranian militants seized the American embassy, suggesting the beginnings of an anti-U.S. regime which, as a matter of convenience, might seek assistance from the Soviet Union.

Second, the USSR invaded Afghanistan suggesting that the Soviets might be trying to fill the power vacuum that existed in Southwest Asia as a result of the fall of the Shah. A growing concern about Soviet power projection capabilitites already existed within the U.S. defense community.[7] The fall of the Shah, the Soviet invasion of Afghanistan and the disaster at Desert One merely reconfirmed—for those who worried about Soviet Third World power projection capabilities—that our traditional focus on European security may not be appropriate for the international environment of the 1980s and 1990s. Furthermore, the fact that most of our West European allies did not see an immediate Soviet military threat to Southwest Asia and believed that they could insure their access to Gulf oil through a variety of political and economic initiatives, did not help matters either.

Third, the Reagan Administration took office in January 1981 and with that change came a significant shift in the strategic focus of U.S. defense strategy. Despite the Carter Administration's early attempts to downgrade the importance of East-West issues and the Soviet-American rivalry, the Carter Pentagon was probably more identified with European continental defense than any other administration in recent U.S. history. The defense of Western Europe—particularly the Center Region of NATO against a short-warning Warsaw Pact attack—dominated the Pentagon's conventional force development planning from 1976–1980. Other theaters were clearly relegated to a secondary status in comparison to European defense. There were even discussions about a "Pacific swing strategy": i.e., in the event of a major war in Europe, some U.S. military forces in the Pacific—primarily naval, but also some air units—would be sent to Europe to help bolster NATO's defenses.

The Reagan Administration came to office convinced that sizing U.S. forces primarily on the basis of the West European contingency was wrong. It believed that the United States faced a global Soviet military threat, and, if war between the United States and the USSR occurred, it most likely could not be contained to a single theater. As a result, DoD planning during the Reagan Administration was based primarily on the assumption that in the event of a major war, the Soviets would attempt to initiate aggressive air, ground, and sea campaigns in multiple theaters in an effort to inflict a massive, global defeat upon the United States and its allies. Generally, DoD's planning scenario, during the Reagan years, assumed that any conflict with the Soviets would start somewhere besides Europe—mostly likely Southwest Asia—and then spread to Europe and the Pacific with major conflicts in each theater. The Reagan-Weinberger Pentagon fundamentally rejected the idea that the Soviets would adopt an operational strategy similar to the one that they had used successfully during World War II: namely, concentrate their military efforts in the area of primary importance and, after success there, move to secondary theaters later—a strategy of sequential rather and simultaneous military operations. As former Secretary of Defense Caspar Weinberger said in 1982:

> A necessary step for the intellectual reform of our policy regarding conventional warfare is to discard artificial definitions and contrived categories—habits of mind that obscure rather than clarify reality. . . .
>
> [A] . . . case in point is the mistaken argument as to whether we should prepare to fight "two wars," "one and a half wars," or some other such tally of wars. Such mechanistic assumptions neglect both the risks and the opportunities that we might confront. We may be focused to cope with Soviet aggression, or Soviet-backed aggression, on several fronts. . . . We cannot settle this question in advance by defining the risk we confront as "one war" or a "war and a half." Moreover, the decision on how large our overall defense effort ought to be must be based on broader and more fundamental judgments than some arbitrary and facile assumption about the number of "wars" or fronts, that we must be prepared for.[8]

Rather than concentrating on a short war in Europe, where winning the first battle was critical, the Reagan Administration proposed to build U.S. capabilities to fight a long, conventional war with the USSR. While no one suggested that losing in the Central Region would be a good idea, a disconcerting string of thought—especially for West Europeans—ran through U.S. defense thinking during the Reagan years. Namely, if the United States were pushed off the European continent, the war would not necessarily be over.

Just a few months before he became Undersecretary of Defense for Policy, Fred C. Ikle argued in *Strategic Review* that Americans should view a war in Europe as one of several campaigns against the USSR. The inference was clear, at least to Europeans: winning individual battles and campaigns are not what is important—the United States did just that in Vietnam. Winning the war is what counts. Ikle seemed to be saying that the United States initially could lose the regional campaign in Western Europe but ultimately win the war with the USSR:

> The Soviet planners should be made to recall the lessons Japan learned after the attack on Pearl Harbor that success in the first campaign does not guarantee a successful ending for a global war.
>
> To be sure, it is not a pleasant prospect for the alliance if its conventional defenses in Europe could be pushed back or overwhelmed by superior Soviet forces while the magic of threatening "first use" of NATO's nuclear arms would fail to restore the status quo. But it is also a highly unpleasant prospect for Soviet planners to envisage that the Soviet Union would still be at war with the United States and other powers, even after a successful conventional campaign in Europe.[9]

In a variety of ways, this theme wove its way through U.S. defense strategy from 1981–1988. Industrial mobilization, surge, sustainability, and reserve component forces were priority issues during the early Reagan defense years, when real defense growth was high. Obviously, if one supports industrial mobilization, surge, sustainability, and reserve forces, this does not imply that he is less interested in West European defense—in fact many of these initiatives would enhance NATO's conventional defense. The issue here is one of emphasis and how the administration felt about where it wanted to invest its marginal dollars, particularly after 1985, when the defense budget stopped growing in terms of real percentage increases: should it hedge against the short-war scenario in Western Europe? If it did, then industrial mobilization and heavy dependence on reserve forces were less important, since U.S. industry could not convert rapidly enough to a war footing to affect a short war and reserve units might not arrive overseas before the war was over. Or, should the administration hedge against a global war where it might be possible to initially lose in one theater—possibly Europe—but ultimately win the war because American industry and reserves would shift the balance of power? The administration chose the latter.

The Reagan Administration's support for the Navy's Maritime Strategy and goals of a 600 ship navy built around 15 deployable carrier battle groups was another indication that the post–World War II consensus concerning the primacy of Europe was in jeopardy. With 15 carrier battle groups, naval spokesman argued that it would be possible to fight simultaneously in multiple military theaters without swinging forces from the Pacific to Europe. More importantly, as the Maritime Strategy evolved in response to its critics,[10] its supporters increasingly settled on an argument quite similar to the one that Ikle had made in 1980. Namely, superior U.S. naval forces could give the United States the capability to fight a "protracted" war with the USSR which was not solely focused on the ground battle in NATO's Central Region.[11]

## Old Wine, New Bottles?

Historically, NATO has weathered numerous crises: Suez, 1956; Berlin, 1961; Mansfield resolutions from 1967 to 1972; the Yom Kippur War, 1973; the enhanced radiation weapons, 1978; the gas pipeline, 1981; and intermediate range nuclear force deployments to name just a few. As a result, it would be easy to say that the spate of NATO bashing in the U.S. press, Congress, and academic journals of recent years is just old wine in new bottles and with good Alliance management, NATO once again can weather the storm. Such a conclusion, however, would seem to be shortsighted for several reasons.

First, NATO's critics are more broad based than in the past. The Mansfield resolutions of the 1960s and 1970s were essentially defeated by a pro-Atlantic "coalition of conservatists and centrists. . . ."[12] Today, however, liberals and conservatives on both sides of the congressional aisle are critical of the current trans-Atlantic relationship. As Tony Coelho, a former House Majority Whip, has said: "You can do ally-bashing now, it's a popular move."[13]

Part of the reason for this attitude is that the issues have moved from more narrow discussions of burdensharing and "free-riding" to include broader concerns of economics and trade. Right or wrong, some Americans are making direct linkages among U.S. deficits, trade imbalances, large defense budgets, and forward deployed troops—not only in Europe but also in the Pacific. There is the perception that our allies are economically more competitive than the U.S. because our alliance partners invest less in defense, freeing large sums of money to invest in domestic industries and giving them a competitive advantage over the United States.[14]

Implicit in these types of arguments is the belief that if the United States spent less on defense it could compete better in the economic market place, and U.S. trade balances and deficits would decline. Until recently, insufficient attention has been given to the possibility that large trade deficits may be the result of structural deficiencies within U.S. industries and the nation as a whole that have little to do with the amount of money the U.S. or its allies spend on defense (for example, inefficient U.S. management practices and theories, tax policies which provide few incentives for long-term investment, antitrust laws that impede cooperative research and development, a national lack of familiarity with foreign languages and culture that undercut American businesses' abilities to penetrate foreign markets or open foreign branch offices, and uneven quality control).[15]

Second, while admittedly impressionistic, the scholarly debate of the 1980s concerning the Alliance seems to be more acrimonious than that of the past and more people seem interested in the debate.[16] More often than not in the 1950s and 1960s, NATO's critics decried the lack of policy consensus within the Alliance.[17] Many of the issues were the same ones we debate today: the role of nuclear weapons, West European conventional contributions to their own defense, out-of-area problems, etc. Nevertheless, as Gregory Treverton has argued, 20 years ago there was a consensus—while not always perfect—about the basic framework: "security concerns predominated and the threat resided in Europe, economics were both secondary and seen as largely cooperative, and strong American leadership, if frequently resented, still was taken for granted."[18] Today, that consensus is in decline.

Even the words that some critics use to describe the Alliance suggest a fundamental animosity, not only toward West Europeans but also NATO itself. For example, Irving Kristol, the neo-conservative publisher of *The Public Interest*, has accused Europeans of adopting a policy of "therapeutic appeasement" toward the USSR and that "the NATO alliance has already been tested—and has been found wanting."[19] In his recent book, Melvyn Krauss was even more critical of the Alliance claiming that "pulling the troops out of Europe may be a little like having surgery to excise a cancerous growth. . . . The signs of cancer already are showing in Western Europe. Why wait until it is too late."[20] Others have claimed that NATO is an "anachronism."[21] Furthermore, it did not help that, while in office, some Reagan Administration officials suggested that Europe was less important in the U.S. security equation, given other competing demands on U.S. resources.[22] One would be hard pressed to find such commentaries about NATO in the 1950s and 1960s.

Third, U.S. leadership within the Alliance is no longer taken for granted. In part, this is natural, and should be welcomed because it demonstrates how successful the effort to rebuild Europe has been. Our allies no longer are economically ravaged, war wrecked economies. In 1950, the United States accounted for more than 45 percent of the world's GNP. [23] Today, America's share of the world GNP (27 percent) is roughly equal to that of NATO-Europe's (20 percent).[24]

One of the down sides of successfully rebuilding the war torn European economies is that even though the United States economic, military, and political potential is larger than any single West European state, our European allies now have significant economic and political interests—inside and outside of Europe—of their own. As sovereign nations, they not only act to defend those interests, which sometimes put them in conflict with us, but also they expect that the United States should recognize that those interests exist. The latter often has been hard for American leaders because implicitly it means some loss of political control and influence within the Alliance. It implies sharing political power and real consultations among allies. It suggests that the United States is not the dominant partner, and, on some issues of concern to the Alliance, it may not even be the first among equals.

Fourth, there is the issue of the new Soviet leadership under Mikhail Gorbachev. It is too soon to make any definitive judgments concerning whether Gorbachev will be successful or not in restructuring Soviet society and transforming the Soviet Union into a more responsible interactional actor. Similarly, there is no consensus among scholars and analysts of the Soviet Union concerning whether or not Gorbachev will be able to retain power and if another reformer or more conservative leader would follow Gorbachev should he fail to achieve his *perestroika* goals in the next five to ten years. But what is clear is that the Alliance faces a more sophisticated—and, as a result potentially more challenging—political leadership in the Kremlin at a time when the NATO consensus is strained.

In the past, Atlanticists could ultimately count on ham-handed Soviet actions to coalesce the Alliance: e.g., invading Hungary or Czechoslovakia, threatening Poland, or an unrelenting conventional and nuclear build-up of Soviet forces in the Central Region. The new Soviet leadership, however, has decided to place greater emphasis—declaratorily at least— on improving the Soviet domestic economy, developing more flexible and sophisticated diplomatic strategies, and supporting the idea of reducing the conventional and nuclear threats in Europe via arms control, as well as by unilateral Warsaw Pact reductions. Such initiatives cannot help but find receptive audiences in European capitals.[25]

Also, as the perception of an immediate security threat from the East declines, due to Gorbachev's "peace initiatives," southern tier NATO states are becoming increasingly worried about the chemical weapon, missile, and general military threat from their regional neighbors to the south. The net result is that developing an agreed upon Alliance strategy, if that is possible, for dealing with a new Soviet leadership and new out-of-area security threats adds another set of burdens to the trans-Atlantic partnership at just the time when many Europeans are questioning American resolve, commitment and leadership abilities in ways that have not happened before.

## Conclusion

NATO's critics have been quite vocal in recent years. As a result, they have captured much of the attention in the public press. However, at this juncture there has been no official wavering on the part of the United States in its commitment to European defense. But should there be some wavering? Given the magnitude of foreign and defense problems confronting the United States, should the Bush Administration consider altering the 40 year old American unilateral guarantee to help Europeans balance Soviet power on the continent?

This is the strategic question that the remainder of this book addresses. The approach is one that should be familiar to students of strategy. It is based on an analysis of ends more than means and the interplay among interests, objectives, threats, and risk assessments. Chapter 2 addresses U.S. interests and objectives, plus an evaluation of the "threat." Chapter 3 examines the historical and future economic, political, and geostrategic importance of Western Europe to the United States. Chapter 4 analyzes the contributions that West Europeans make to their own defense and evaluates the strategic implications associated with various proposals favoring a unilateral reduction in the U.S. military presence in Europe that have been advocated in recent years. Chapter 5 outlines a set of policy issues and decisions that NATO needs to pursue, in order to bolster the American commitment and strengthen the trans-Atlantic partnership as NATO enters the 1990s—its fifth decade of existence.

# 2

## U.S. Strategy and the Role of Europe

Any attempt to understand America's role in NATO and why Europe should continue to be the priority region of importance in U.S. national security planning must begin with a discussion of strategy. As trite as this may seem, all too often this basic fact is forgotten or conveniently overlooked and analysts proceed immediately to a discussion of U.S. and NATO Force Goals; the state of the static or dynamic military balance; what weapons we should or should not buy; or, worse yet, to a discussion of the most appropriate tactical or operational campaign plan that NATO should adopt. These issues are not unimportant. But, they make sense only in the context of broader policy and strategy issues. Therefore, this chapter goes back to the basics and reviews the role of policy and strategy in U.S. national security affairs; changes in the strategic environment; U.S. interests and objectives; Soviet military threats to U.S. interests and objectives; and the proper interplay among threats, interests, objectives and force deployments.

### Policy and Strategy

Strategy is the exercise of making difficult choices among competing demands. In the current era, the basic challenge facing the United States is: Can we continue to protect our vital interests in Europe without jeopardizing interests in other regions of the world and accomplish both of these goals while not increasing the risk of nuclear war?

If money were a free object and it were possible to buy everything that we needed for national defense, there would be no need for strategists or regional priorities. But money is not free and national defense is expensive—as some of the critics of NATO are more than delighted to point out. More importantly, if it were possible to buy everything that was needed to cover all threats, defense planning and strategy could be performed by accountants, not strategists. The reality is, however, that the strategist's world is very similar to that of the economist. Economists deal with scarcity, and strategists know that in a democracy like our own, they will never obtain all the needed resources to cover all threats.

As a result, strategists must make choices. Based on the guidance received from political decisionmakers, strategists must establish priorities in an attempt to balance unconstrained desires with what is feasible, practical and within the risk parameters that political decisionmakers are willing to accept. Or, as Robert Komer has argued, "strategy . . . [is] the art of making sound choices—or putting first things first."[1]

This is clearly a difficult agenda, at any time. However, it is even more complicated when the United States faces a period of slow or zero real growth in its defense budgets. However, it is an agenda that can be accomplished. But, to make it achievable, we will have to keep the relationship between policy and strategy clearly in mind.

In the United States at least, the central feature of national security affairs is that policy must dominate process. Policy establishes the political objectives that strategy must achieve. Policy lays out the political context within which strategy must operate; i.e., it establishes the limits or bounds. Strategy, on the other hand, is the plan of actions designed to achieve policy goals and objectives in light of threats, interests and opportunities. Strategy considers all the components of national power: economic, political, socio-psychological, and military. As a result, military strategy is only one aspect of national strategy; and, more importantly, a military strategy that is not in harmony with economic, political, and socio-psychological plans of actions ultimately cannot succeed.

Even though it is common place to hear pundits argue that U.S. policy, goals, objectives, and strategy are episodic—changing regularly with every new administration—in reality the basic outlines of U.S. policy have changed very little since the start of the twentieth century. The basic U.S. policy is relatively simple, clear cut, but immensely sensible and that is why it has endured through at least 11 presidential changes. What is that policy? Simply put, that the United States does not want to see a hostile state or group of states dominate the Eurasian landmass—the area which Mackinder called the world's heartland. We fought two world wars to prevent Germany from dominating the military and industrial potential of Europe because if this had occurred, the world balance of power would have shifted against American interests. And, since 1945, we have attempted to prevent the USSR from capitalizing on its geostrategic location to dominate its neighbors in Europe, Asia, and the Middle East and thereby alter the global balance of power to our disadvantage.

The strategy to achieve this policy has been containment in the fullest sense that George Kennan meant when he coined the concept. Administrations have differed over whether they should emphasize "offensive" or "defensive" containment strategies, "symmetrical" or "asymmetrical" responses to Soviet actions, and which instruments—economic, military, or political—should receive the most attention.[2] But, in the final analysis, for more than 40 years, every administration—be it Republican or Democratic, conservative or liberal—has endorsed the concept that U.S. strategy, out of necessity, must prevent the Soviet Union directly or indirectly from dominating the industrial and military centers of Europe and Asia. The major military elements of this strategy have been forward deployment, coalition defense, and an explicit linkage between U.S. nuclear forces and European defense—a guarantee that requires sufficient survivable U.S. nuclear capabilities to withstand a Soviet nuclear first strike and still be able to inflict unacceptable damage upon the USSR.

The point of this discussion is not to argue that U.S. policy or strategy for the last 40 years has been wrong. Rather, it is an attempt to demonstrate that, indeed, there has been a large amount of coherence to U.S. policy and strategy! As a result, those who advocate altering the character of the American commitment to European defense are proposing more than merely pulling U.S. forces out of Europe. They are advocating a major change in U.S. strategy. And, more importantly, in reality they are proposing a shift in U.S. policy—a policy that not only has stood the test of time but also has survived multiple changes in administrations during this century. If policy drives strategy, then we should change policy before we change the strategy or strategies that have been fostered to implement policy decisions. Major alterations that affect our ability to implement the strategy could result in a *de facto* change in policy which is exactly how the policy-strategy equation should not function. A fundamental question then is: Has the strategic environment changed so dramatically that U.S. policymakers should abandon old approaches and adopt radically new ones?

## Strategic Environment

For nearly 40 years, U.S. policy and strategy has been based upon a particular set of strategic concepts. These concepts include: nuclear deterrence (based on mutual vulnerability and assured destruction), escalation control, forward deployment of U.S. forces in areas deemed to be important to the United States, conflict control (i.e., a desire to limit the geographic scope, intensity, and duration of any conflict), and crisis management. These concepts were developed when the United States was the world's preeminent nuclear power and had a clear technical and, qualitative advantage in strategic, theater and battlefield nuclear weapons. In addition, these concepts and the resulting military strategies to execute them were developed when U.S. alliances were relatively cohesive and the United States was believed to be not only the military, but also the political and economic leader within the Western world.

Events in the 1970s and 1980s clearly demonstrated that changes in the strategic environment have occurred. First, the United States no longer has strategic nuclear superiority. Since at least the mid-1970s, a rough equivalence in strategic nuclear weapons has existed between the two superpowers, although significant asymmetries in particular delivery systems exist.

Second, Soviet conventional military capabilities have improved. The USSR is militarily involved in areas of the world where it never has been previously. The Soviet Union still is inferior to the United States in conventional global power projection capabilities; however, its exploitation of events in Angola, Ethiopia, and Afghanistan in the 1970s and 1980s contrast sharply with its ineffective attempts to use its military forces for political purposes in the Congo in the 1960s and Peru in 1970. Nevertheless, through most of the 1990s, Soviet power projection capabilities will continue to be constrained because of three traditional limiting factors: (1) an imbalance between naval logistical support ships and combatants that limit how long Soviet combatants can be deployed at sea; (2) a mechanized and tank heavy Army which gives the USSR certain advantages in the European theater, but is very difficult to deploy, sustain, and support in theaters noncontiguous to the USSR; and (3) a lack of reliable friends and allies who want to see Soviet military presence consolidated within their countries. In addition, it seems that Moscow may have decided that its policy of active military adventures in the Third World during the 1970s led to few political rewards. In fact, it appears that the USSR may pursue a less active military role in the Third World, at least for the immediate future.

Nevertheless, the simple fact is that Soviet ships, planes, or advisers have been in a particular country or deployed in areas of the world where they have not been located traditionally. This changes the level of risk that today's American political decisionmakers must be willing to accept before committing the U.S. military to action. Even though it is possible to demonstrate that the Soviet Union lacks the ability to support and sustain conventional military operations in most noncontiguous theaters—except against very unsophisticated adversaries—Soviet capabilities to deploy significant forces to distant regions have altered the way that many American strategists and policymakers view the strategic environment. This perception alone is significant, even if the "hard" facts would argue that Soviet power projection capabilities have been exaggerated and recent "soft" assessments envision a less adventuresome USSR in the immediate future.

Third, U.S. alliances are not as cohesive as they formerly were. In part, this is because the United States is no longer the sole political and economic leader of the Western world. The growing economic strength of Western Europe, Japan and the other Pacific rimland states, and the oil-rich nations of the Persian Gulf/Middle East have caused those nations to pursue not only more assertive independent economic policies, but also to challenge the United States in the international political arena.

The current weaknesses in the U.S. alliance system also result from legitimate differences in outlook among sovereign nations over what are the best ways to obtain competing national interests. Simply put, our allies do not always perceive the "threat" in the same way that the United States does, because their interests and objectives are different from ours. This does not mean, as one critic of NATO has argued, "that American and allied [NATO] perceptions of the Soviet Union are so different that one must ask whether Washington and the allies continue to agree that there is in fact a Soviet threat to the West."[3]

NATO allies—and other allies as well—recognize a Soviet threat. In recent years, however, they have been less inclined to accept unquestioningly that the American response is the right or only way to react. The prevailing perception of a monolithic communist threat, which was the basis of the U.S. post–World War II military alliance system (NATO, CENTO, SEATO, and a sundry of bilateral agreements), no longer has the credibility that it did in the 1950s or even the 1960s. As a result, alliance consensus is more difficult to forge and more fragile to maintain than in the past.

Finally, the disintegration of the post–World War II bipolar environment has caused not only a more diversified fragmented world, but also a more interdependent one. A primary result of the general diffusion of economic, political, and military power that has occurred over the last 40 years is the inability of both superpowers to control and shape events to the degree that they would like. This phenomenon has been amply exhibited in the volatile and important region of Southwest Asia during the 1970s and 1980s. Despite its efforts, the United States was unable to curb the indigenous uprising that led to the fall of the Shah of Iran. Likewise, the Soviet Union lacked the ability in Egypt or Somalia to keep those strategically important countries from expelling Soviet forces and ultimately could not defeat the poorly organized, but fierce fighting Afghan Mujihadeen freedom fighters. While neither superpower approves of nuclear proliferation, it continues to occur in the Middle East, South Asia, and Southwest Asia even though some of the participants are ostensibly "friends and allies" of the United States and the Soviet Union. A similar situation exists with chemical weapons. Washington's and Moscow's inability to influence the protracted war of attrition between Iran and Iraq, although neither superpower's interests were advanced by the conflict, is just another example of how difficult it is for the superpowers to control events, even when they are occurring in a strategically important region.

Moscow and Washington are not impotent. However, in a strategic environment where the primary causes of regional conflicts are more often than not indigenous with historical roots that have little relationship to East-West competition, where both superpowers are dependent upon raw materials and products from the politically unstable Third World, and where alternative arms suppliers and a growing indigenous Third World arms production capability exists, traditional superpower power crisis management tools (e.g., show of force, increasing or cutting off arms, etc.) are becoming less effective. The web of global interdependence often makes strange bedfellows as witnessed by the fact that adversaries like Israel and Syria provided arms and other assistance to Iran, as did even the United States, during the Iran-Iraq war.

Most analysts can agree that the strategic environment has changed. Many can even agree on how it has changed and what are the salient characteristics of the new environment. However, it is at this point where the consensus begins to unravel. There is virtually no agreement for how the United States should react or what solutions it should attempt to adopt to cope with the new strategic environment. For example, Samuel Huntington has argued that the traditional U.S. strategic concepts "are of dubious relevance to the conditions of the 1980s."[4]

Other critics of current U.S. strategy have argued that the global strategic center of gravity has shifted from Europe and Northeast Asia to the Persian Gulf and the other resource-rich Third World nations requiring a refocus of U.S. military strategy and forces toward those regions.[5] There is another group of strategists who essentially argue that the United States no longer can afford economically to support its global presence and world-wide commitments. As a result, they recommend sometimes radical changes in U.S. strategy and force deployments to bring commitments into line with their projections of what will be economically feasible in the future.[6] Finally, there is a group of strategists who recognize the importance of the Third World, but believe, as does Robert Komer, that an overemphasis upon preparing and sizing U.S. forces for lesser contingencies in the Third World makes the United States a prisoner of the "fallacy of the most likely argument." In other words, the United States may acquire the capability to deal with Grenada "liberations," Iran hostage raids, or countercoup attempts in a myriad of countries, but ultimately fail to prepare adequately for the defense of what is most vital to the United States—protection of the European political, economic, and military heartland. This latter group believes that traditional U.S. strategy and its underlying concepts are basically sound. Therefore, they support making the strategy more effective through better alliance cooperation rather than changing it.[7]

Has the strategic environment changed so much the United States should revamp its basic strategy? Obviously, there is no easy answer to this basic question. Otherwise, the heated strategic debate that has been ongoing throughout most of this decade would have cooled long ago. Clearly some things have changed: strategic nuclear equality, improved Soviet power projection capabilities, global economic and political interdependence, and the rise of a multi-polar versus bi-polar world, to name just a few.

However, many of the so-called dramatic changes in the strategic environment were predictable, are irreversible and, in fact, were fostered by U.S. policy. For example, the United States sponsored, supported, and encouraged West European and Japanese economic revitalization after World War II in the belief that economically prosperous allies were more politically stable and that this best served U.S. interests and objectives. In the short term, the relative decline in America's economic and political status is disconcerting to some observers. Nevertheless, it would be difficult to support an argument that the United States would be better off today if Europe and Japan were as economically weak and vulnerable as they were in the 1950s. The only real opportunities that the USSR has been able to exploit in the post–World War II period have been in those countries which were weak, isolated, and vulnerable. And, now it appears that Moscow may have come to the conclusion that it did not achieve much from its activist policies in the Third World during the 1970s.[8]

Europe and Japan may not follow U.S. leadership to the same degree as they did in the 1950s or to the extent that some American analysts and politicians would prefer. However, neither has any desire to see Soviet political power consolidated in their region of the world or anywhere else for that matter. In that regard, not only has the strategic environment not changed but also two of the world's most important economic and political power centers are better able to resist the USSR which helps the United States obtain its most important post–World War II objective—containing the spread of Soviet influence and power.

Another area where there has been no significant change to the strategic environment is in the area of superpower conflict avoidance. Since the end of World War II—even before Moscow obtained nuclear weapons—a tacit understanding between the two superpowers existed:

namely, direct Soviet-American conflict had the possibility of escalating out of control—a situation which neither Moscow nor Washington found appealing. Despite some critics' claims to the contrary, the principle of superpower conflict avoidance still seems to affect Soviet policy. If anything, under the Gorbachev regime, the Soviets have pushed the issue of superpower conflict and crisis control—because of the risks associated with nuclear war—even more to the forefront in their political statements, rejecting claims made in the 1960s and 1970s that if war (to include nuclear war) occurred the USSR would prevail.

By far the most important aspect of the strategic environment that has not changed is geography and its effect on U.S. national security policy. The United States is unique in the history of global powers. Unlike any other great power in history, the United States virtually is immune to conventional invasion. Geography and the historical circumstances of weak military powers on our immediate borders and vast oceans to our east and west make it impossible for any conceivable adversary to conquer and occupy the United States. Our nation's survival can be threatened, and is by strategic nuclear weapons. However, for more than 150 years our territorial integrity has not been threatened. More importantly, there are no plausible scenarios that project such a threat anytime in the near future. If we face any threat from our neighbors, it is a threat of weak, economically vulnerable neighbors on our southern border.

Partly because we face no immediate military threats to our territorial integrity, those economic, political, and military interests and objectives that are most important to the United States are located in other parts of the globe—far from the American continental borders. As a result, the United States must not only have the capability but also be perceived to have the political will to project *power*—not just military power but political, economic, technological, and socio-psychological power as well—to protect its interests and objectives.

In the military arena then, the United States is much like Great Britain of the late nineteenth and early twentieth centuries. The United States is primarily a reinforcing power. We depend upon allies and coalitions of like-minded states to help us achieve our interests and objectives. Classic balance of power concepts, as a result, undergird our foreign and national security policies. To forge the types of alliance relationships that a reinforcing power like the United States needs to achieve its interests and objectives often require a non-transitory military commitment. Such military commitments in effect are a promise from a reinforcing power that it will forsake its geographic opportunity—or luxury—and become engaged in distant political and military events. A reinforcing power—like the United States today or Great Britain in the nineteenth century—must take such actions because it ultimately cannot be secure if other countries or areas of the world that are important to it are threatened. Ground forces stationed in a region or country historically have been recognized as the strongest signal of a reinforcing power's commitment to carry out its obligations in crisis or should deterrence fail.

## Interests and Objectives

The fundamental building blocks of strategy are the concepts of national interests and specific objectives to support the attainment of national interests. From national interests should flow a national strategy: a plan for how to employ a nation's military, political, economic, psychological, and technological tools to achieve interests and objectives. Out of that national strategy should arise a specific military strategy—or strategies—to support the national strategy. The military strategy should guide the creation of forces and operational strategies that are consistent with the national strategy.

There are four fundamental categories of national interests common to all sovereign nations: survival, territorial integrity, maintenance or enhancement of economic well-being, and a favorable world order (see Table 2.1). The United States is a unique nation in that it is virtually invulnerable to a conventional invasion. However, its survival is threatened by the immense nuclear capacity of the USSR. Fortunately, the Soviet Union is no less vulnerable to a nuclear attack, even under conditions of nuclear parity, and this reality has led the Soviets to avoid direct military confrontations with the United States because of fears that uncontrolled escalation might result from such situations.[9]

Nevertheless, conflict avoidance or not, strategic choices among the major categories of national interests must still be made. Clearly in order of priority, survival and protection of territorial integrity are the most vital interests of any nation and actions that jeopardize these interests should not be entered into lightly or haphazardly. There is legitimate debate among strategists over how one should rank the latter two national interests. I tend to believe that U.S. economic interests should receive third priority, and world order interests—such as stability, democracy, human rights, etc.—should receive fourth priority. The primary reason for this is a recognition that in many regions of the world the norm is political instability. As a result, rather than adopting a national goal to eliminate instability, which more often than not is caused by indigenous factors over which the United States or any outside power has very little control, the United States may have to learn to accept it in many instances. Besides, some changes in the status quo are not that bad. At

**Table 2.1**
**GLOBAL INTERESTS BY REGION**

| Category | Region | |
|---|---|---|
| | Western Hemisphere | West Europe |
| Survival | • Deterrence of nuclear war | • Deterrence of nuclear war |
| | • Nonproliferation | • Nonproliferation |
| Territorial Integrity | • Defend air and sea approaches to North America | • Maintain integrity of NATO nations |
| | • Protect U.S. bases and territory | • Protect U.S. bases |
| Economic well-being | • Retain access to critical raw materials and markets | • Maintain and expand trade and investments |
| | • Maintain and expand trade routes | • Continue free passage over international air and sea |
| Favorable world order | • Peaceful resolution of conflict | • Prevent extension of Soviet influence in Europe |
| | • Prevent extension of Soviet influence | • Maintain U.S. credibility and regional influence |
| | • Prevent drug trafficking | • Deter conventional war in Europe |
| | • Combat terrorism | • No hegemony in regions hostile to the United States |
| | • Keep conflicts local | • Keep conflicts local |
| | | • Combat terrorism |

the national level, U.S. policy should be based on managing change rather than being rigidly fixed to preserving the status quo in many Third World areas.

Before leaving the concept of national interests, there are a few more important attributes of national interests that should be mentioned. First, not all national interests are of uniform importance nor should they be pursued with equal intensity. For example, it is clearly more important that the United States avoid direct military conflict with the Soviet Union over peripheral issues because of the strategic nuclear risks inherent with superpower conflict than it is to cause the East European empire to break apart—as much as we might like to see the latter occur. However, avoiding the risks associated with nuclear war directly relates to national

**Table 2.1**
(Continued)

| | Region | | |
|---|---|---|---|
| Category | Southwest Asia/Middle East | East Asia & Pacific | Africa South of Sahara |
| Survival | • Deterrence of nuclear war | • Deterrence of nuclear war | • Deterrence of nuclear war |
| | • Nonproliferation | • Nonproliferation | • Nonproliferation |
| Territorial Integrity | | • Defend Hawaii and Alaska and U.S. bases and territory | |
| | • Protect U.S. bases and territory | • Protect U.S. bases | • Defend air and sea approaches to North America |
| Economic well-being | • Deter attacks on sources of raw materials and associated sea lines of communication | • Maintain and expand U.S. trade and investments | • Maintain and expand trade and investments |
| | • Retain access to oil region facilities | • Retain access to natural resources of region | • Retain access to natural resources of region |
| Favorable world order | • Promote U.S. trade and investments | • No hegemony in Northeast Asia hostile to the United States | • Maintain U.S. credibility and regional influence |
| | • Combat terrorism | | |
| | • Firm defense of Israel | • Maintain U.S. credibility and regional influence | • Prevent extension of Soviet influence |
| | • Limit Soviet influence | | • Combat terrorism |
| | • Maintain U.S. credibility and regional influence | • Improve relations with People's Republic of China | • Keep conflicts local |
| | • Settle Arab-Israel conflict without losing moderate Arab support | • Reduce threat of Communist insurgency | |
| | | • Combat terrorism | |
| | • Keep conflicts local | • Keep conflicts local | |

survival interests while fostering the breakup of the Warsaw Pact is a world-order objective.

There are a number of ways to express intensity of interests.[10] One method is to define interests as vital, significant, important or of interest.[11] Vital interests are those goals or events which decisionmakers believe are so critical that they would be willing to risk escalation to nuclear war to obtain or preserve. As the term implies, a vital interest is essential for self-preservation. One should think about vital interests in the same manner as medical doctors think about vital or life sustaining organs. If a nation does not obtain these interests or objectives, it ceases to live or have a quality of life that is meaningful. As mentioned earlier, every administration since the turn of the century—and particularly since the end of World War II—has subscribed, declaratorily at least, to the idea that it is in America's national security interests to see that the Eurasian land mass is not physically dominated or intimidated by a power hostile to the United States. In the next chapter, we will discuss in more detail some of the economic and socio-political reasons for this intensity of interest in Europe.

Significant interests on the other hand, are those goals and objectives which the United States would be willing to risk the use of military force, but not nuclear weapons, to obtain. Important interests are less critical than vital or significant interests, but are of sufficient importance that air, naval, logistical, and even ground forces—the latter probably only in an advisory mode—would be employed to facilitate their attainment. Finally, things that are of interest are not significant enough to risk war over. This does not mean that they are unimportant. Rather, in the grand scheme of national strategy, it means that to obtain them we would use diplomacy, aid, technical and humanitarian assistance, etc., rather than military forces.

Second, interests not only are pursued with less than uniform vigor, but also they are often in competition with one another. For example, in Southwest Asia, the industrial world's need for Persian Gulf oil requires that access be assured, and this access, in turn, requires the support of moderate Arab states. The U.S. commitment to Israel is a complicating factor in achieving the required Arab support, which Europeans and the Japanese have more than once pointed out to U.S. policymakers.

Third, national interests may also be direct or indirect. Hypothetically, if Western Europe is a vital interest of the United States, then Persian Gulf oil fields and sea lines of communications between the Persian Gulf and Western Europe would also be a vital interest of the United States, albeit indirectly. Another example is Korea. If Korea is considered to be vital to the defense of Japan, and if Japan is vital to U.S. economic well-being, Korea then is an indirect vital interest of the United States. Other interests may derive from the satisfaction of these indirect interests: Korea is now also important to the United States quite apart from its relationship to the defense of Japan because of significant American economic investments there. This latter case illustrates the need to periodically review the basis of a nation's stated national interest in a particular country or region to see if conditions have changed the parameters of the relationship.

Finally, in some cases national and international interests have become indistinguishable. For example, the national interests not only of the United States and the Soviet Union but also of all nations of the world require that general nuclear war between the superpowers be avoided. It is even possible that in some areas the concept of parochial national self-interests may be vanishing in a world where increasing interdependence and technological advances in weapons and destructive power make it dangerous for nations to pursue national interests with military means.

## Interests, Objectives, Plus Threats

To argue that we do not want to see the Eurasian landmass physically dominated or intimidated by a power hostile to the United States—in one way of looking at things—is not the answer to a problem, but rather explains the challenge that the U.S. decisionmakers face. As a global power we have political, economic, and military interests in a variety of regions. As a result, those critics of NATO who implicitly—and in some cases explicitly—argue that the United States must choose between Europe and the Far East miss the point. We should not have to choose. Both regions are important—maybe even vital—to the United States. As Table 2.1 indicated, to a major degree our interests and objectives in both regions are similar. We want to: deter hostile attacks upon the United States and our allies; be in a position to defeat aggressors if deterrence fails; ensure U.S. and our major allies access to markets and raw materials; and strengthen and, to the degree possible, enhance U.S. influence throughout the world. If this is the case, the factors that should affect U.S. force deployments then are not interests and objectives only but rather interests and objectives plus threats.

There are a myriad threats to U.S. interests. In the coming decade the United States will face numerous challenges in the Third World and other regions of the world that will be only marginally related to or caused by the USSR. Nevertheless, there is no doubt that the Soviet threat will continue to be the most significant military threat against which defense planners will judge strategic, force structure and deployment decisions.

The reasons why the USSR will continue to dominate U.S. defense planning should be obvious, but are worth repeating. First, through the use of strategic nuclear weapons, the USSR is the only nation in the world capable of threatening American survival. Second, even if the Soviet Union follows through on its offer to reduce its forces and alter their offensive capabilities, the USSR will most likely still retain the largest modern military force in the world. Third, no matter what is the final outcome from the Conventional Forces in Europe (CFE) negotiations, the Soviet Union will continue to border on the regions of the world that the United States believes are most important to it. If those regions were ever politically or militarily dominated by a power hostile to the United States, a major shift in the world balance of power would occur. Fourth, despite some of Moscow's appealing declaratory overtures in recent months, there are no immediate changes on the horizon in either Soviet deployments or force structure that will change the fact that the Soviet Union will continue to be the dominant political and military threat to U.S. interests and objectives.

Nevertheless, it is important to remember that the Soviet military threat is not uniform or universal against all U.S. strategic interests. As just mentioned, the Soviet Union can threaten U.S. survival through the use of strategic nuclear weapons. Despite the claims of a few pundits, however, there is no real evidence to suggest that Moscow believes that it can fight and win a strategic nuclear war with the United States. In fact, in his recent book, Michael MccGwire has built a powerful case that Soviet strategic objectives changed in the 1970s from "destroying the capitalist system" with all the attendant risks associated with a nuclear war that came with such an objective to "gravely weakening the capitalist system" which could be achieved preferably through nonnuclear means, if war should ever occur.[12] The risks of attempting to "destroy the capitalist system" (i.e., the United States) were just too great even for the most wishful Soviet planner. Therefore, as long as the USSR does not obtain a first-strike capability and the United States continues to guard against Soviet technological breakouts in ballistic missile defense that would invalidate nuclear deterrence, the idea of constraints on the use of military force and superpower conflict avoidance should remain intact. In regard to U.S. territorial integrity, Soviet forces pose no significant threat. U.S. geostrategic location continues to make it virtually immune either to conventional invasion or occupation. On the other hand, the Soviet threat to U.S. economic and world order interests is more diverse. But the most significant Soviet military threat for the foreseeable future will continue to reside in Europe, even if conflict there is less likely to occur than in other regions.

Over the last two decades, the Kremlin has made significant strides in improving its overall military capabilities. Nevertheless, the USSR is still primarily a European, land-oriented continental power. It looks at the world through a European prism, and, even more than the United States, the European contingency has determined Soviet force structure and doctrinal requirements. Soviet ground, naval, and air forces all reflect a defense establishment that is dominated by army and continental-oriented officers.[13] Soviet emphasis on armored divisions and mechanized combined-arms teams, speed, mobility, preemption, unit replacement, large mobilizeable reserves to augment understrength peacetime divisions, preplanned tactical air strikes to extend the range of artillery, limited combat radii for tactical aircraft, poor ratio of fleet support ships to combatants—which adversely affects Soviet power projection and naval sustaining capabilities—and a navy that still needs land-based air forces to protect its ships are attributes of a military structure that is tailored primarily with a European land battle in mind.

Given this set of circumstances, it is not surprising that the majority of Soviet forces are deployed against NATO countries. More importantly, however, Soviet military deployments demonstrate a clear sense of regional priorities. Those regional priorities in order of importance are Europe, the Far East—particularly China—and Southwest Asia. Correspondingly, the military deployments that flow from those regional priorities translate into rather specific types of threats to U.S. interests and objectives. Some are more severe than others and, as a result, demand appropriate responses.

Before turning to look at how the Soviet Union currently deploys its forces and then offering an assessment of the Soviet threat if Gorbachev's 1988 unilateral reductions are carried out, we need to underscore two major caveats. First, the assessments that follow are purely static—a quantitative "bean count" if you will. Obviously there are more so-phisticated methodologies to employ: e.g., armored divisional equivalents, weighted firepower scores for various military units, dynamic gaming assessments, comparative rates of mobilization potential, etc. However, for our purposes, whether one uses static or more dynamic measures the ultimate conclusion will be the same: the most severe Soviet/Warsaw Pact military threat currently lies in Europe. The exact numbers of that military threat may change as a result of unilateral Warsaw Pact reductions or the successful conclusion of a CFE agreement but for the immediate future the majority of Soviet capabilities will reside in Europe. Soviet capabilities in the Far East are circumscribed by geography and other geopolitical factors of which the most important is Chinese animosity toward the USSR. From a Soviet perspective the military balance in Southwest Asia does not look as favorable as western analysts often assume and, as a result, regional conflicts and internal instabilities—that the Soviets will try to take advantage of—are more of a threat to U.S. interests than the possibility of a massive Soviet invasion.

Second, we are not attempting to argue that there is no Soviet threat in regions that are non-contiguous to the USSR. Rather, we are suggesting that in regions like Africa, Latin America, and even large parts of Asia, the Soviet Union poses more of a political, subversive, nonmilitary threat to U.S. interests and objectives because Soviet force structure factors establish their own set of constraints on Kremlin decisionmakers. As a result, U.S. responses should be tailored to these types of threats which in many cases do not require significant deployments of active military forces.

## Current Soviet Deployments

*NATO-Europe.* Three Soviet land theaters of military operations (TVDs) and naval forces from the Atlantic, Baltic, Black Sea Fleets and Mediterranean Ocean Squadron have operational missions against NATO. The Northwestern TVD's area of operation in war would include Norway, as well as Sweden and Finland. The Western TVD—which includes East European forces from East Germany, Poland, and Czechoslovakia; Soviet forces in each of those Warsaw Pact nations; and Soviet forces from the Baltic, Belorussian and Carpathian military districts—are oriented toward NATO's Central Region. The Southwestern TVD includes Soviet and East European forces from Bulgaria, Rumania, and Hungary and Soviet forces from the Kiev and Odessa military districts. This TVD has a wartime mission to execute military operations against NATO's southern flank, including Italy. The Moscow, Ural, and Volga military districts comprise the Soviet Union's central strategic reserve. Divisions from these three military districts could be committed to any TVD. However, more often than not, when committed in Soviet exercises, they are allocated against NATO's Central Region.

When fully mobilized, the Western TVD commander would have at least 63 Warsaw Pact ground (31 tank, 30 motorized rifle and 2 airborne) plus 6 artillery divisions, and 2,000 tactical aircraft, over 19,000 main battle tanks, and 16,300 artillery, multiple rocket launchers, and heavy mortars.[14] Thirty-three general purpose submarines, 180 naval aircraft, and 50 major surface combatants from the Baltic Fleet would have the mission to support either Western TVD operations by executing operations against the German and Danish coasts or Northwestern TVD operations against the southern coasts of Scandinavian countries.

The Northwestern TVD upon full mobilization could field 11 motorized rifle, 1 airborne and 1 artillery divisions; 1,350 main battle tanks; 2,100 artillery pieces, multiple rocket launchers, and heavy mortars; and 160 combat aircraft. Ground operations against North Norway could be supported by an additional 227 naval aircraft, 126 general purpose submarines, and 73 major surface combatants from the Soviet Northern Fleet.

Finally, after mobilization, a Southwestern TVD commander would have the following Soviet forces available: 29 divisions (10 tank, 18 motorized rifle, and 1 airborne) plus 3 artillery divisions; and over 7,700 main battle tanks; 6,000 artillery pieces, multiple rocket launchers, and heavy mortars; and over 860 combat aircraft. The Black Sea Fleet and Mediterranean Ocean Squadron could support operations against NATO's southern flank with approximately 35 general purpose submarines, 80 major surface combatants, and 460 naval combat aircraft.

*Southwest Asia.* Soviet forces in the North Caucasus, Trans-Caucasus, and Turkestan military districts are part of the Southern TVD's operational command and pose the most immediate threat to Southwest Asian nations. The major forces available to a Southern TVD commander are 30 divisions (1 tank, 27 motorized rifle, and 2 airborne); and approximately 5,400 main battle tanks; 5,700 artillery pieces, multiple rocket launchers, and heavy mortars; and 700 combat aircraft. In war, the Indian Ocean Squadron—possibly augmented by additional ships from the Pacific Fleet—would support operations in Southwest Asia.

*Far East.* The Far East TVD is geographically the largest of the USSR's land TVDs. It encompasses more than half of the USSR, incorporating the Central Asian, Siberian, Transbaykal, and Far Eastern military districts and Mongolia. With up to 57 maneuver divisions (7–8 tank, 48 motorized rifle, and 1 airborne) plus 5 artillery divisions; approximately 14,900 main battle tanks; 13,700 artillery pieces, multiple rocket launchers, and heavy mortars; and 1,300 combat aircraft, it is second only to the Western TVD in military capabilities. In the event of war, the Far Eastern TVD ground and air operations would be supported by assets from the Pacific Fleet: 92 general purpose submarines, 75 major surface combatants, 560 naval combat aircraft, and a naval infantry division.

## Soviet Threat After Proposed 1988 Unilateral Reductions

Attempting to make any exact predictions concerning what the Soviet or Warsaw Pact threat may look like over the next two years (the period in which Gorbachev claimed that the USSR would carry out its unilateral cuts) to five years is extremely difficult. The West is being nearly overwhelmed with Warsaw Pact unilateral offers to reduce its forces. In just a little over a month after Gorbachev's December 1988 UN speech, the German Democratic Republic announced a 10,000 man, 600 tank, 50 fighter aircraft reduction. Poland has claimed that it will cut its defense budget by as much as 40 percent. The Hungarian Defense Minister claimed that Hungary would reduce its forces by 251 tanks, 430 artillery pieces, and 1 squadron of combat aircraft. Czechoslovakia has indicated that it will reduce its forces by 850 tanks, 165 armored vehicles and 51 combat aircraft and Bulgaria has announced a 10,000 man, 200 tank, 200 artillery, and 20 aircraft reduction.[15] Over the next several years—particularly if CFE talks bog down over issues such as data exchanges and whether or not to include NATO's naval forces in the negotiations—NATO must expect more unilateral offers from the Soviets and East Europeans.

Clearly, Gorbachev is trying to send the following message to the West European publics: the Soviet threat is declining or will decline in a significant sort of way in the future. While this may happen, it will be imperative for Western leaders clearly to articulate to their publics that unilateral Warsaw Pact offers to reduce their forces are welcomed, but military stability within Europe at lower force levels ultimately can be achieved only through negotiated reductions that can be verified.

NATO has been burned in the past. For example, in 1979, Leonid Brezhnev announced the unilateral withdrawal of the 6th Guards Tank Division from the Group of Soviet Forces Germany. It took the West nearly two years to discover that the division's headquarters was returned to the USSR but the division's personnel and equipment were largely redistributed throughout Eastern Europe. The net result being a one division reduction in the Soviet Union's forward deployed force structure but an overall increase in the capabilities and readiness of its other divisions in Eastern Europe.

NATO and individual members of the Alliance must avoid becoming caught in a seductive trap of making separate counter offers to appear "responsive" to Gorbachev. The Soviets and the Warsaw Pact have just too much "excess" capacity to play with in this type of game. As a result, they can offer what appear to be significant cuts without giving up an overall advantage. Alliance counter responses can never look as impressive. For example, the Soviet Union's recent offer to cut its tank forces in the forward areas by 5,300 tanks would equal about a 50 percent reduction in the Soviet tank inventory in its Groups of Forces in Eastern Europe. Eliminating 10,000 Soviet tanks would equal a 22 percent reduction in the overall Warsaw Pact tank threat. After such a cut, however, the Warsaw Pact would retain over 19,000 tanks in the Western TVD oriented toward NATO's Central region—2,500 more tanks than currently are in all NATO units. In addition, there would be more than 20,000 other tanks throughout Eastern Europe and the Soviet Union oriented toward NATO nations.[16] In other words, if NATO did nothing in response to the Warsaw Pact's recent offers, a 12,751 Warsaw Pact tank cut would leave NATO still outnumbered by more than 2.4:1. Also, NATO would still be at a 2.4:1 and 1.8:1 disadvantage in artillery and combat aircraft (see Table 2.2).

On the other hand, if NATO decided to reduce its tanks forces as some sort of good will gesture, a 50 percent reduction (over 8,000 tanks) would not equal Gorbachev's major reduction offer of 10,000 tanks. A 30 percent reduction (4,927 NATO tanks) would not equal the USSR's forward subzone offer of 5,300 tanks. Or put another way, *NATO could eliminate the total tank inventories of Belgium, Netherlands, France, United Kingdom, Denmark, Norway, Portugal, Canada, and Spain and not obtain a 5,000 tank reduction.* Such radical cuts would probably spell the demise

TABLE 2.2
**IMPACT OF WARSAW PACT UNILATERAL REDUCTION OFFERS\***
(AS OF FEBRUARY 1989)

|  | TANKS | ARTILLERY | COMBAT AIRCRAFT |
|---|---|---|---|
| **WARSAW PACT** | | | |
| TOTAL | 51,500 | 43,400 | 8,250 |
| SOVIET | 37,000 | 33,000 | 6,050 |
| **REDUCTIONS** | | | |
| SOVIET | 10,000 | 8,500 | 800 |
| NSWP | 2,751 | 630 | 130 |
| **NEW TOTAL** | 38,749 | 34,270 | 7,320 |
| **NATO (EXCLUDES US POMCUS AND REINFORCEMENTS)** | 16,424 | 14,458 | 3,977 |
| **FORCE RATIO BEFORE CUTS** | 3.1:1 | 3.1:1 | 2.1:1 |
| **WITH JUST SOVIET CUTS** | 2.5:1 | 2.4:1 | 1.9:1 |
| **WITH SOVIET & E. EUR CUTS** | 2.4:1 | 2.4:1 | 1.8:1 |

\* EQUIPMENT IN UNITS ONLY

SOURCE: NORTH ATLANTIC TREATY ORGANIZATION, *CONVENTIONAL FORCES IN EUROPE: THE FACTS* (BRUSSELS, BELGIUM, NATO INFORMATION SERVICE, 1988).

of initial defense in Europe, leaving only a nuclear tripwire to deter attacks.

The point here is a simple one: the Soviets can, and most likely will, continue to manipulate their vast military resources to affect public threat perceptions. The United States and its Alliance partners to some degree are hamstrung given that equal cuts would be militarily irresponsible. As a result, conventional arms control that leads to major asymmetrical reductions on the part of the Warsaw Pact—particularly Soviet unit and equipment levels—and brings the Warsaw Pact more in line with NATO force levels is still the best path for the Alliance to follow.

Soviet withdrawal and reduction proposals, however, could result in a Warsaw Pact threat that to some degree would be slower building, making Soviet force posture more in line with the Soviet Union's political view of how a war in Europe would most likely come about: a prolonged period of political tension on the continent preceded by a significant decline in superpower relations. This is an important factor for European and American military and force development planning. But a Soviet capacity to generate significantly more forces in a shorter period of time—i.e., a disparity in mobilization capability—could still exist, even after a negotiated CFE agreement. This is particularly the case when one considers that movement times for Soviet reinforcing forces, after they are trained in the Western Military Districts, are usually calculated in days, whereas the U.S. reinforcing times are in weeks and months. This disparity could be even more pronounced given western democracies historical reluctance to mobilize in crisis, particularly if the United States would decide to withdraw some of its forces from Europe prior to the signing of a conventional arms control agreement.

Thus, American and European leaders will ultimately have to convey to their publics and parliaments that a negotiated conventional arms control agreement will not eliminate the Warsaw Pact threat. A good agreement might change the character and timing of the threat, but it will not alter the requirement for prudent levels of defense expenditures in the future. Failure to invest and build an adequate deterrent posture after the euphoria of a CFE agreement—if one can be signed—could leave Europe in a more unstable military position than it is now.

## Conclusion

What does all this mean? Four conclusions seem obvious. First, U.S. policy and strategy have not been episodic. There has been a great amount of consistency in the basic outlines of U.S. policy and strategy during this century. Before we change those policies and strategy, we should be sure that changes are warranted. Second, the strategic environment has changed. However, not as much as some observers believe. Third, we have competing interests and objectives. But, there is nothing new to this phenomenon. The strategic issue is how does the United States balance those competing interests and objectives in light of the military threats that it confronts.

Finally, and most important, the Soviet Union currently has more than 200 divisions to allocate against its perceived threats and opportunities. Fifty percent of those divisions—not including the Central Reserve military districts—are allocated against NATO. If one includes the Moscow, Volga, and Ural military districts, then 59 percent of the Kremlin's available divisions are allocated against NATO. Thirty percent of its divisions—over 40 percent including the Central Reserve—are allocated against NATO's Central Region. Moreover, 63 percent of the Soviet Union's Category I divisions have missions against NATO countries.[17]

Of the more than 50,000 Soviet main battle tanks and 40,000 artillery, multiple rocket launchers, and heavy mortars, currently in the Soviet total inventory more than 50 percent—nearly 60 percent including the Central Reserve divisions—face NATO nations; over 35 percent of Soviet tanks and 30 percent of its artillery are in the Western TVD directly threatening NATO's Central Region. Despite recent growth in the Soviet Far East Fleet, which has been a major concern of the last two Secretaries of Navy,[18] the USSR still deploys over 70 percent of its general purpose submarines, 70 percent of its principal surface combatants, 75 percent of its amphibious ships, and 66 percent of its naval aircraft in fleets and squadrons directly oriented against NATO nations' navies, shipping and sea lines of communications.

All of this means that a significant military threat to Europe still exists—a threat that is different from that which exists in other regions of the world. Also, as Table 2.2 indicated, even if Moscow follows through on its offers to reduce its forces unilaterally, a major Warsaw Pact military threat will continue to exist in Europe. Even if our interests and objectives in Europe were only equal to those in other regions— which is not the case and will be developed more fully in the next chapter—the United States would want to forward deploy a significant number of forces in Europe in order to counter the military threat that it faces and to protect its interests and objectives. With this discussion of interests, objectives, plus threats as a background, it is now time to examine in more detail why Western Europe continues to be geostrategically, economically, and culturally important to the United States.

# 3

# The Strategic Importance of Europe to the United States

In the last chapter we addressed the issue of the interrelationship between threats and interests. While that discussion was brief the message is clear: a significant Warsaw Pact military threat to Europe still exists and will most likely continue to exist, despite unilateral Soviet offers to reduce its forces and adopt a more defensive doctrine and force posture. The majority of Soviet forces, currently and in the future, will be deployed against NATO—particularly against the Central Region. From those deployments, it is relatively easy to deduce that Moscow continues to believe that Western Europe is the strategic prize in its global competition with the United States. While war in Europe may be the least likely of a variety of potential conflict scenarios, the military threat is real, will continue to exist and, if deterrence should fail, the consequences would be significant, given the risks of nuclear escalation.

At the same time, however, Chapter 2 argued that threats alone should not determine U.S. policy and strategy. Policy and strategy should be based on the interplay between interests, objectives and threats. A major problem in American history has been that too often this interaction at the policymaking level has not occurred. As John Lewis Gaddis has argued so correctly, "threats . . . [all too often have] been allowed to determine interests, rather than the other way around."[1] If decisionmakers allow only threats to drive policy and strategy, they will become the prisoner of their adversaries' actions. Policy and strategy will become reactive rather than deliberate and forward looking because the decisionmaker and strategist will have no independent standards to measure U.S. security and threats against other than the "threat" or the presence or nonpresence of an adversary's forces in a particular area or region of the world.

The following analysis challenges the assumption of some NATO critics that in the future Europe will not be as important to the United

States as it once was. Also, it challenges the view that NATO-Europe's current strategic value to the United States has changed as other areas—particularly Southwest Asia and the Far East—have grown in significance over the last decade.[2]

Several of NATO's critics fundamentally view the world, as well as U.S. interests and objectives, as a zero-sum game. If some region or country grows in importance, then that means some other country or region must become less important to balance the strategic question. The strategic process just does not work that way, however. To argue that Southwest Asian oil or the burgeoning industrial potential of the East Asian rimland states like Japan, Korea, Taiwan, South Korea have grown in importance does not mean that Europe is any less important to the United States. It simply means that in comparison to *themselves* a few years ago, these areas and nations have moved up on the hierarchy of interests. This does not necessarily mean, however, that Europe has moved down. Moreover, Europe, as will be developed in more detail later, is still economically, geostrategically, and culturally important to the United States *and is militarily threatened in a serious way.* Southwest Asia and the Far East's economic importance has increased, *but they are not threatened in the same way as is Europe.* These are important, but often overlooked, distinctions.

The remainder of this chapter will analyze why Europe should to continue to remain the primary region of strategic importance to the United States. Chapter 2 discussed the military threat and it will not be addressed any further here. This chapter will examine the economic importance of Western Europe to the United States in comparison to other regions; Europe's geostrategic importance (to include some thoughts on what it could mean geostrategically if the USSR controlled Europe or through intimidation politically dominated Western Europe); and current and future American ancestral, cultural and historical ties to Western Europe.

Some analysts might question the inclusion of ancestral heritage in a strategic assessment, so let's briefly explain why it will be discussed. As was mentioned in Chapter 2, one of the four broad national interests common to all nations is the desire to create a favorable world order.[3] For the United States, at least, that favorable world order is founded on principles of democracy, the rule of law, and the protection of individual and human rights. As a nation, we believe that these principles can be best advanced through cooperation with nations and peoples that share similar concerns. If there is one region of the world, more than any other over a longer period of time, that historically has shared this American political philosophy, it is the democracies of Western

Europe from which the United States predominantly traces its democratic, constitutional, and historical origins.

As a result, ancestral, historical, and cultural ties are important. They help to create a common bond and perceptions among regions of the world that reinforce political, economic, and military ties. These perceptions are reflected in American public opinion polls. For example, a recent Chicago Council of Foreign Relations poll indicated that 70 percent of the American public and 85 percent of the "leaders" believed that the United States should either increase or maintain its military presence in Europe at current levels. Sixty-eight percent of the public favored sending American troops to Europe, if the Warsaw Pact invaded. However, only 53 percent of the public supported sending troops to Japan, if the USSR invaded that country, and 24 percent of the public favored reinforcing South Korea with American forces, if it were invaded by North Korea. Furthermore, as a place of postgraduate study for their children, American leaders overwhelming favored Europe to Asia (69 percent versus 15 percent).[4]

## Economics

In the fall of 1986, then Secretary of the Navy John Lehman is reported to have argued that changing U.S. trade patterns in combination with the growth of the Soviet Pacific Fleet should cause the United States to think about altering its traditional regional priorities raising the Pacific to at least equal status with Europe.[5] In January 1988, Secretary of the Navy James H. Webb, Jr., picked up his predecessor's theme and went even further arguing that the U.S. should "zero base" its military commitments and avoid "post-INF thinking that conventional forces in Europe be increased . . . , or for that matter such a buildup should occur in Europe at all, or even that it be a land-oriented build-up." Why? Because U.S. economic commitments in the Pacific were growing as was the Soviet threat.[6]

Clearly, U.S. trade with Asia has increased significantly over the last 15–20 years. This is a major reason why not only former Secretaries Lehman and Webb but also other observers believe that the United States should alter its traditional defense planning regional priorities. However, when one looks at more than just import and export figures— e.g., total gross national products; foreign direct investment in the United States and U.S. direct investment overseas; and development assistance to promote economic growth in poorer countries—Europe for the foreseeable future should still remain as the priority region in the United States national security planning.

TABLE 3.1
## TRADE AS PERCENTAGE OF TOTAL DOLLAR VALUE

|  | 1967 | | 1984 | |
| --- | --- | --- | --- | --- |
|  | WESTERN EUROPE | ASIA* | WESTERN EUROPE | ASIA* |
| U.S. MERCHANDISE EXPORTS | 31 | 28 | 27 | 33 |
| U.S. MERCHANDISE IMPORTS | 30 | 23 | 22 | 42 |
| U.S. MANUFACTURED EXPORTS | 29 | 15 | 24 | 25 |
| U.S. MANUFACTURED IMPORTS | 38 | 25 | 24 | 48 |
| U.S. AGRICULTURAL EXPORTS | 36 | 36 | 27 | 37 |

*    JAPAN TO MIDDLE EAST, EXCLUDES
     AUSTRALIA AND NEW ZEALAND

SOURCE:  U.S. DEPARTMENT OF STATE, BUREAU OF PUBLIC AFFAIRS, *ATLAS OF THE UNITED STATES FOREIGN RELATIONS,* (WASHINGTON, DC:  U.S. GOVERNMENT PRINTING OFFICE, 1985), pp. 58-59.

*Trade.* Table 3.1 demonstrates that a major shift in U.S. trade patterns has occurred over the last 20 years. U.S. trade with Asia exceeds that with Europe in all categories.

Two caveats relating to the figures in Table 3.1 are worth mentioning, however. First, these figures do not include Canada which is our single largest trading partner. If U.S. foreign and defense policy were determined by economics alone, we would draw a defense perimeter around Canada and forget the rest of the world. Also, Canada is a member of NATO. Therefore, to the extent that one looks at our trade with Canada as part of the larger NATO/European picture, the European trade figures would appear significantly different. For example, trade with Western Europe plus Canada would be equal to or exceed trade with Asian countries in every category, except manufactured imports and agricultural exports. And, in each exception, there would be only a five percent difference between Asia and Western Europe plus Canada.

Second, an over emphasis upon trade as an indicator of U.S. interests can ignore that not *all* trade is necessarily positive. Our trade balance with both Western Europe and Asia is negative, but it is worse with Asia. For example, in 1985, for every dollar of merchandise and man-ufactured goods that we sold to Western Europe we brought in $1.36 in imports. For Asia, the ratio was nearly 1:2.25. In the specific case of Japan, the ratio of imports to exports—prior to the 1987 trade sanctions—was 1:3.30.[7] Suffice it to say, while trade with Europe might be smaller, it is more balanced. As should be obvious from recent congressional sentiment, overly negative trade balances can contribute to alliance dissension rather than cohesion.

TABLE 3.2
# SHARES OF WORLD GROSS NATIONAL PRODUCT BY REGION

| WESTERN INDUSTRIAL | PERCENTAGE |
|---|---|
| UNITED STATES | 27 |
| NATO EUROPE | 20 |
| CANADA | 2 |
| TOTAL NATO | 49 |
| JAPAN | 9 |
| OTHER EUROPE | 3 |
| | |
| WARSAW PACT | |
| | |
| SOVIET UNION | 14 |
| NON-SOVIET WARSAW PACT | 4 |
| TOTAL WARSAW PACT | 18 |
| | |
| THIRD WORLD | |
| | |
| LATIN AMERICA | 5.5 |
| AFRICA | 3 |
| MIDDLE EAST | 3 |
| SOUTH ASIA | 2 |
| EAST ASIA (LESS JAPAN) | 5 |

SOURCE:   Derived from data in RUTH LEGER SIVARD, *WORLD MILITARY AND SOCIAL EXPENDITURES, 1987-1988* (WASHINGTON, DC: WORLD PRIORITIES,1987), pp.43-45.

*Factors Other Than Trade.* A more balanced picture of Europe's economic importance must include other factors than just trade. For example, as Table 3.2 indicates, a Europe that for whatever reasons came under Soviet influence would more than double the Soviet economic potential. To equal NATO-Europe's potential, politically or militarily Moscow would have to control or influence not only Japan but also East Asia, South Asia, the Middle East and Africa. The latter is clearly beyond Soviet military capabilities. Conquering Europe may be also, but it is in the range of realistic possibilities.

The economic importance of Europe, in comparison to other regions of the world, is also reflected in the level of U.S. direct investments in European nations and vice versa as compared to Asia. In 1984, U.S. private direct investment in Europe amounted to over $104 billion or 47 percent of U.S. investment abroad. Asia, Japan, and the Middle East totalled no more than 11 percent of U.S. private direct investment abroad. On the other hand, Western Europe accounted for 67 percent ($107 billion) of the foreign direct investment in the United States whereas Japan equalled only 9 percent ($15 billion).[8] The loss of Europe, therefore,

TABLE 3.3
OFFICIAL DEVELOPMENT ASSISTANCE BY DEVELOPMENT ASSISTANCE
COMMITTEE MEMBERS, 1983

| MEMBERS | % OF GNP | NET DISBURSEMENTS ($ MILLIONS) |
|---|---|---|
| NETHERLANDS | 1.08 | 1,195 |
| SWEDEN | 1.02 | 754 |
| NORWAY | .99 | 584 |
| DENMARK | .76 | 395 |
| BELGIUM | .59 | 480 |
| AUSTRALIA | .56 | 753 |
| FRANCE | .49 | 2,500 |
| GERMANY FEDERAL REPUBLIC OF | .48 | 3,176 |
| CANADA | .41 | 1,429 |
| UNITED KINGDOM | .37 | 1,605 |
| AUSTRIA | .35 | 157 |
| FINLAND | .30 | 153 |
| JAPAN | .28 | 3,761 |
| NEW ZEALAND | .28 | 61 |
| UNITED STATES | .27 | 7,992 |
| SWITZERLAND | .25 | 320 |
| ITALY | .24 | 827 |
| TOTAL DAC | | 26,142 |

SOURCE:   U.S. DEPARTMENT OF STATE, BUREAU OF PUBLIC AFFAIRS, *ATLAS OF UNITED STATES FOREIGN RELATIONS*, p. 70.

would have a devastating impact on private U.S. investors as well as the entire American economy.

This is not to say that Japan or other rimland Asian states coming under Soviet influence or domination would have no influence on the U.S. economy. Quite the contrary would be true. In comparison, however, the loss of Europe would have a greater impact.

Another indicator of Western Europe's importance to the United States is its willingness to assist Third World countries through developmental assistance. As a nation, the United States tends to believe that efforts to raise the standard of living and develop the economies of Third World countries contribute to international peace and stability—objectives consistent with our world order interests. If we look at NATO-Europe's contributions to developmental assistance as a total rather than as individual contributions, our West European allies make a rather significant contribution in this area.

For example, as Table 3.3 indicates, the United States and Japan provide the largest numbers of dollars to Third World nations. However, in terms of percentage of GNP devoted to Third World developmental assistance Washington and Tokyo rank near the bottom. As a result, the relative burden and thereby financial commitment to Third World development and stability by countries like the Netherlands, Federal Republic of Germany, Canada, and United Kingdom is considerably greater than they are often given credit for. In 1983 dollars, our West European allies—including France—provided $10.8 billion in developmental assistance whereas the United States and Japan provided $8 billion and $3.8 billion respectively. In other words, NATO-European states, less France, provided over twice as much to developmental assistance as did Japan. If one includes France, the ratio is 2.9:1. Moreover, NATO-Europe's contribution, less France, to Third World developmental assistance exceed U.S. efforts by $270 million. NATO-Europe, plus France, surpassed the United States by more than $2.7 billion.

## Geostrategic Location

Those who favor altering the U.S. military commitment in Europe have a point: just as much as alliances enhance U.S. security, they also can detract from it. In the nuclear age, if the ultimate occurs and by force of arms the United States must defend its alliance commitments against Soviet incursions, the United States ultimately could be destroyed.[9] Alliance partners also can draw America into conflicts that it would prefer to avoid.

Before writing off the geostrategic importance of Europe, however, one must recognize, as Colin Gray has so aptly pointed out, "some geopolitical considerations of enduring relevance for the very structure of American security" that the NATO alliance provides.[10] Even some of those observers who favor altering the American relationship with NATO have recognized this fact. For example, Robert Tucker has argued that one of the possible consequences associated with the withdrawal of U.S. forces from Europe, if Europeans do not fill the gap, would be to free the Soviet Union to concentrate in other areas and thereby increase American risks elsewhere.[11]

NATO allows the United States to participate in the control of the most important Soviet exits to the world: the Bosphorus and Dardanelles, Gibraltar, Skagerrak and Kattegat, and the North Norway approaches to the Atlantic. The significance of this should not be downplayed or misunderstood.

Should the USSR ever gain control or influence over these major exit points, the United States—and Europe too—would confront a more dangerous world. From good historical experience, the Soviets understand that exits to the world can equally be used as hostile invasion routes. As a result, to a large degree, Soviet military strategy is focused on employing its forces to defend or prevent adversaries from using these traditional "choke points" for hostile actions directed against the Soviet homeland.[12]

If Soviet forces which are now dedicated to "defensive missions" were ever freed, the geostrategic implications could be profound. Moscow's ability to project power in the Third World could be enhanced. But more importantly, NATO's ability to control events, if a European war occurred, would be severely complicated. Rather than forced to concentrate on an area sea denial strategy, Moscow could decide to adopt a more aggressive open-ocean anti-SLOC (sea lines of communication) campaign, which U.S. and NATO planners currently do not envision nor plan aggressively against.

In addition, we should keep in mind that geography will force the USSR to consider the risks associated with a multi-front war, as long as NATO exists as a viable military alliance. Over the last six to eight years the virtues and detriments of horizontal or geographic escalation have been debated extensively. Generally, given the constrained military assets available to the Alliance, in the event of conflict I can find few strategic or operational advantages that accrue to the United States if it does not concentrate its forces at the primary point of tension or conflict. Hopefully, after success in the most important regions, the United States would then focus its efforts on secondary theaters. Once deterrence fails, seizing Cuba, Angola, Viet Nam, Nicaragua, etc. makes little sense, if such activities do not contribute in a direct way to defeating the USSR in Europe, or Southwest Asia or the Pacific—if one of the latter is Moscow's main theater of attack.[13]

Recognizing the practical limitations associated with executing a horizontal escalation strategy and even realizing that there may be few reasons why the United States and its allies would consciously want to expand a regional crisis into a global war, however, does not reduce the problem for Kremlin planners. Geography and the existence of NATO require Moscow's planners to consider such a possibility. These realities contribute to deterrence. They also may go a long way toward explaining why Gorbachev has decided to adopt a more conciliatory approach toward the West for the time being.

For example, assume for the moment that the Kremlin intends to invade Iran. How could a Soviet military planner assure his political bosses—with a high level of confidence—that eventually NATO would not become engaged? Even if no forces in Eastern Europe were put on alert, which is highly unlikely given the extremely conservative nature of Soviet military planners, an invasion of Iran would threaten Turkey. Some of the forces that Moscow would want to use against Iran are also part of the Southwestern TVD and oriented toward Turkey in the event of a NATO war. If Moscow failed to commit these forces against Iran, it could jeopardize its chances for success.[14]

On the other hand, if the initial preconflict mobilization steps to bring Soviet low readiness divisions near Turkey's eastern border up to strength were noticed, Turkey and NATO would not know whether those forces were being prepared for an invasion of Iran or Turkey. Maybe NATO would respond as an alliance and deploy the European AWACs, Allied Command Europe (ACE) Mobile Force, or other air and ground forces as preconflict deterrent actions. If NATO failed to act, however, it is possible that Turkey would request bi-lateral U.S. military assistance, possibly AWACs, training teams, advisers, and security assistance. If the United States honored such requests, particularly if it agreed to provide AWACs coverage until the crisis clarified, this could mean that as many as four AWACs, several fighter squadrons, and ground security forces to protect the AWACs might be deployed to Turkey. Needless to say, in either case the stakes would be raised and the potential for escalation horizontally and vertically would be increased.

The point of this discussion is *not* to argue that the United States or NATO should abandon the idea of limiting the scope of regional conflicts. This element of our strategy has served us well for the last 40 years. Rather, it is an effort to demonstrate that the geostrategic location of certain NATO states presents Kremlin planners with some unique problems. A prudent Soviet military planner would have to think through this type of scenario before recommending the use of military force to achieve Soviet objectives. And, the inability to confidentially predict the outcome of a series of ill-defined events is one of the basic tenets of deterrence.

## Cultural Heritage

Cultural heritage and ancestral roots, by themselves, will not ensure a U.S. military and political commitment to Europe. But, they will play some role in determining American attitudes toward Europe. As one German soldier has so accurately stated, it is the American public's attitude toward Europe—of which heritage and ancestry are important elements—that could decide "the continuation of the U.S. commitment to Europe in peacetime."[15]

Demographic trends and their impact on American perceptions and commitment toward Europe are a mixed bag. To some degree, how one interprets these trends is based on whether one views the proverbial glass as half-full or half-empty. For the immediate future, however, the trends are positive in Europe's favor.

TABLE 3.4
## FOREIGN-BORN PERSONS IN THE U.S. BY COUNTRY/REGION OF BIRTH

| REGION/COUNTRY | FOREIGN-BORN PERSONS |
|---|---|
| | (1,000) |
| EUROPE | 4,743.6 |
| ASIA | 2,539.8 |
| CENTRAL AND SOUTH AMERICA | 4,383.9 |
| CANADA | 842.9 |
| USSR | 406.0 |

SOURCE:   U.S. DEPARTMENT OF COMMERCE, BUREAU OF THE CENSUS, *STATISTICAL ABSTRACT OF THE UNITED STATES, 1987*, 107TH ED. (WASHINGTON, DC:  U.S. GOVERNMENT PRINTING OFFICE, 1987), p. 37.

Table 3.4 indicates some of the negative or pessimistic factors. The total legal immigrant population in the United States is approximately 14.1 million: 4.7 million come from Europe; 2.5 million are from Asia; and nearly 4.4 million come from Central and South America. More significant is the timeframe when the largest portion of the immigrants arrived in the United States. More than 65 percent of the Europeans came before 1960—largely as result of immigration bursts following World Wars I and II. In contrast, 69 percent of the Asian and over 40 percent of the legal Central and South American immigrants arrived in the United States during the 1970s.

These are the types of statistics which cause many observers to be concerned. Will such demographic trends and patterns ultimately cause a shift in American strategic focus: a shift away from Europe and toward Latin America and Asia? On the positive side—at least for those like this author who continue to believe that there are good strategic reasons to maintain a strong political and military commitment to Europe—these negative trends are counterbalanced by data such as found in Tables 3.5, 3.6, and 3.7. Based on 1979 U.S. Census Bureau data, NATO nations account for 50 percent of the Americans claiming single ancestry. If one takes into consideration all of Europe—minus the Soviet Union—58 percent of the American population claims single ancestral roots to Europe. In comparison, not quite 2 percent of Americans claim single ancestral roots to Asian countries. When allowed to choose only a single ancestry, approximately 8 percent of the American population claims its ancestral roots from Latin American countries.

**TABLE 3.5**
**AMERICANS REPORTING SINGLE ANCESTRY**

| ANCESTRY | PERSONS REPORTED SINGLE ANCESTRY | |
|---|---|---|
| | NUMBER | PERCENT |
| REPORTED AT LEAST ONE SPECIFIC ANCESTRY | 96,496 | 100 |
| AFRO-AMERICAN, AFRICAN | 15,057 | 15.6 |
| AMERICAN INDIAN | 2,053 | 2.1 |
| ASIAN INDIAN | 156 | 0.2 |
| AUSTRIAN | 385 | 0.4 |
| BELGIAN | 113 | 0.1 |
| CANADIAN | 228 | 0.2 |
| CHINESE, TAIWANESE | 540 | 0.6 |
| CZECHOSLOVAKIAN | 794 | 0.8 |
| DANISH | 438 | 0.5 |
| DUTCH | 1,362 | 1.4 |
| ENGLISH | 11,501 | 11.9 |
| FILIPINO | 525 | 0.5 |
| FINNISH | 255 | 0.3 |
| FRENCH | 3,047 | 3.2 |
| FRENCH CANADIAN | 582 | 0.8 |
| GERMAN | 17,160 | 17.8 |
| GREEK | 567 | 0.6 |
| HUNGARIAN | 534 | 0.6 |
| IRANIAN | 103 | 0.1 |
| IRISH | 9,760 | 10.1 |
| ITALIAN, SICILIAN | 6,110 | 6.3 |
| JAMAICAN | 158 | 0.2 |
| JAPANESE | 529 | 0.5 |
| KOREAN | 230 | 0.2 |
| LEBANESE | 179 | 0.2 |
| LITHUANIAN | 317 | 0.3 |
| NORWGIAN | 1,232 | 1.3 |
| POLISH | 3,498 | 3.6 |
| PORTUGUESE | 493 | 0.5 |
| RUMANIAN | 132 | 0.1 |
| RUSSIAN | 1,496 | 1.6 |
| SCANDINAVIAN | 110 | 0.1 |
| SCOTTISH | 1,615 | 1.7 |
| SLAVIC | 300 | 0.3 |
| SPANISH | 9,762 | 10.1 |
| COLUMBIAN | 101 | 0.1 |
| CUBAN | 558 | 0.6 |
| DOMINICAN | 107 | 0.1 |
| MEXICAN | 5,889 | 6.1 |
| PUERTO RICAN | 1,107 | 1.1 |
| OTHER SPANISH | 2,000 | 2.1 |
| SWEDISH | 1,216 | 1.3 |
| SWISS | 312 | 0.3 |
| UKRAINIAN | 231 | 0.2 |
| VIETNAMESE | 177 | 0.2 |
| WELSH | 455 | 0.5 |
| WEST INDIAN | 129 | 0.1 |
| YUGOSLAVIAN | 283 | 0.3 |
| OTHER SPECIFIED ANCESTRY GROUPS | 2,372 | 2.5 |

SOURCE: U.S. DEPARTMENT OF COMMERCE, BUREAU OF CENSUS, *ANCESTRY AND LANGUAGE IN THE UNITED STATES: NOVEMBER 1979*, SPECIAL STUDIES SERIES, P. 23, NO. 116 (WASHINGTON, DC: U.S. GOVERNMENT PRINTING OFFICE, 1982) p. 7.

If one allows Americans to report multiple ancestry as Table 3.6 does, then the ancestral ties to Europe are even more profound. In 1980, nearly three-fourths of the American population claimed to be some combination of German, Irish, or English descent.

What about the future? As Table 3.7 indicates, the White/non-Hispanic portion of the U.S. population is expected to decline during the twenty-first century and the Hispanic, Asian, and Black portions of the American population will grow, significantly in the case of Hispanics. However, if the ancestral claims noted in Table 3.6 continue—and there is no reason to expect that they should change dramatically—on NATO's 100th

TABLE 3.6
**AMERICANS REPORTING MULTIPLE ANCESTRY**

| NATION | PERCENTAGE OF THOSE REPORTING ANCESTRY | PERCENTAGE OF THOSE REPORTING MULTIPLE ANCESTRY |
|---|---|---|
| GERMAN | 28.8 | 66.8 |
| IRISH | 24.4 | 77.7 |
| ENGLISH | 22.3 | 71.3 |
| AFRO-AMERICAN, AFRICAN | 9.0 | 7.0 |
| SCOTTISH | 7.9 | 88.6 |
| FRENCH | 7.8 | 78.3 |
| ITALIAN, SICILIAN | 6.6 | 48.0 |
| AMERICAN INDIAN | 5.3 | 79.3 |
| POLISH | 4.7 | 58.5 |
| DUTCH | 4.5 | 83.2 |
| MEXICAN | 3.7 | 11.9 |
| SWEDISH | 2.7 | 75.1 |
| NORWEGIAN | 2.3 | 70.1 |
| "OTHER SPANISH" | 2.1 | 43.9 |
| RUSSIAN | 1.9 | 56.8 |
| WELSH | 1.4 | 82.3 |
| CZECHOSLOVAKIAN | 0.9 | 53.2 |
| DANISH | 0.9 | 73.8 |
| HUNGARIAN | 0.9 | 66.5 |
| PUERTO RICAN | 0.7 | 17.0 |
| SWISS | 0.7 | 74.6 |
| AUSTRIAN | 0.6 | 64.0 |
| FRENCH CANADIAN | 0.6 | 44.7 |
| GREEK | 0.6 | 42.7 |
| LITHUANIAN | 0.5 | 61.9 |
| PORTUGUESE | 0.5 | 47.9 |

SOURCE: DONALD J. BOGUE, *THE POPULATION OF THE UNITED STATES: HISTORICAL AND FUTURE PROJECTIONS* (NEW YORK: THE FREE PRESS, 1985), P. 376. COPYRIGHT © 1985 BY THE FREE PRESS, A DIVISION OF MACMILLAN, INC. REPRODUCED BY PERMISSION OF THE PUBLISHER.

anniversary over 140 million Americans, at a minimum, will claim Europe as part of their heritage. In other words, Americans claiming European ancestral heritage will outnumber those claiming Hispanic culture by 2.8:1; Black by 2.7:1; and Asian and other races by 7.6:1.[16] Obviously, none of this means that any racial or cultural group automatically will endorse U.S. security policies or interests in Europe by the middle of the twenty-first century. Race, cultural, linguistic background, or ancestral roots alone will not determine how *all* Americans view our security relationship with Europe. Nevertheless, one should not denigrate the fact that 65 years from now the vast majority of Americans will still have strong historical, cultural and ancestral ties to Europe and with those ties will come a level of commitment that may be difficult to quantify but will still exist.[17]

## Conclusion

As the above analysis indicates, Western Europe continues to be extremely important to the United States. If one is predisposed to pessimism or a desire to change the American relationship with Europe,

TABLE 3.7

TOTAL POPULATION, BY RACE AND SPANISH ORIGIN: 1982 TO 2080

(AS OF JULY 1, 1986, NUMBERS DO NOT SUM TO TOTAL BECAUSE THE SPANISH ORIGIN MAY BE OF ANY RACE. NUMBERS IN MILLIONS.)

| YEAR | TOTAL | SPANISH ORIGIN | WHITE NON-HISPANIC | BLACK | OTHER RACES |
|---|---|---|---|---|---|
| 1982 | 232.1 | 15.8 | 183.5 | 27.7 | 5.9 |
| 1985 | 238.6 | 17.5 | 186.8 | 29.1 | 6.4 |
| 1990 | 249.7 | 19.9 | 192.0 | 31.4 | 7.5 |
| 1995 | 259.6 | 22.6 | 196.2 | 33.7 | 8.5 |
| 2000 | 268.0 | 25.2 | 198.9 | 35.8 | 9.5 |
| 2010 | 283.2 | 30.8 | 202.6 | 40.0 | 11.7 |
| 2020 | 296.5 | 36.5 | 204.5 | 44.2 | 13.7 |
| 2030 | 304.8 | 41.9 | 202.4 | 47.6 | 15.6 |
| 2040 | 308.6 | 46.7 | 197.2 | 50.3 | 17.3 |
| 2050 | 309.5 | 50.8 | 190.8 | 52.3 | 18.9 |
| 2060 | 309.7 | 54.2 | 184.8 | 53.7 | 20.4 |
| 2070 | 310.4 | 57.2 | 180.0 | 54.9 | 21.9 |
| 2080 | 310.8 | 59.6 | 176.0 | 55.7 | 23.4 |

SOURCE:   U.S. DEPARTMENT OF COMMERCE, BUREAU OF THE CENSUS, *PROJECTIONS OF THE HISPANIC POPULATION: 1983-2080,* POPULATION ESTIMATES AND PROJECTIONS SERIES P-25, NO. 995 (WASHINGTON, DC: U.S. GOVERNMENT PRINTING OFFICE, 1986), p.10.

it is still possible to find examples within these statistics to support such views. However, this chapter demonstrates that a more comprehensive view of the situation suggests that this is not the only, or even the most plausible interpretation one should reach.

The U.S. has a negative trade balance with West European states. However, the trade pattern is not as out of balance as the one which exists with East Asian nations. In other economic areas, like developmental assistance to Third World nations, Western Europe out performs not only the United States but also Japan. Even though immigration from other areas of the world is increasing, the vast majority of the American population will continue to trace its ancestral roots to West European nations and culture for the foreseeable future.

Demonstrating that Western Europe is still important to the United States and faces a more significant military threat than other regions of the world are not sufficient reasons alone, NATO's critics argue, to continue deploying over 350,000 American forces in the region. Europeans must spend money for their own defense. If Europeans are unwilling to make the commitment and financial sacrifice to help defend themselves, some of NATO's critics argue that the U.S. should rethink its unilateral commitment to participate in the defense of Western Europe, given the inherent nuclear risks associated with that commitment. The next chapter examines the contributions that West Europeans make to their defense.

It addresses some of the risks and strategic implications—not only for the United States but also for our European allies and allies in other regions of the world—if the United States were to decide to withdraw a substantial portion of its forces from the European theater prior to a CFE agreement.

# 4

## The Contribution of Western Europe to Its Own Defense

Most critiques of NATO and recommendations that the United States should reevaluate its policies toward the Alliance stem from a belief that Europeans can do more for their own defense, but choose not to. As a result, NATO's critics tend to argue that the United States not only pays a disproportionate cost for Europe's defense but also risks its survival through Flexible Response when Europeans do not seem as concerned about the Warsaw Pact threat.

Depending on the author, the argument may be phrased diplomatically or eloquently such as Brzezinski has done: "The painful fact is that Europe continues to suffer from historical fatigue, induced by the shattering effects of two colossally destructive wars. The initial positive impetus to create an integrated Europe tied to America quietly waned, once the immediate post–World War II economic misery had been relieved and once the seeming urgency of the Soviet military threat had been offset by America's enduring commitment to Europe's security. It became convenient to disengage from America's global competition with Russia while continuing to benefit from America's regional protection."[1] Or, they may be more blunt. For example, Jeffrey Record has argued that "by almost any standard of peacetime military performance, key European allies—notably Germany and the Low Countries, where most U.S. forces in Europe are stationed—are failing to do their part for their common defense. . . . [T]hey still devote to their own defense a far smaller portion of their national wealth than does the United States, whose borders are not menaced by a Group of Soviet Forces Canada or Group of Soviet Forces Mexico."[2] And, Melvyn Krauss has said "the fact that detente has become Europe's second 'line of defense' against the Soviet Union—behind the U.S. guarantee—is a very dangerous development for the United States. . . . One result of Europe's detente-as-strategy, then, is that the United States must spend more on its own defense because the Europeans are adding resources to the Soviet war-machine."[3]

Whether stated diplomatically or bluntly the argument is essentially the same. Europeans are seeking a "free ride." They are unwilling to invest in their own defense. They want the twin benefits of military security—provided mostly by the United States—and economic prosperity. However, the critics argue that Europeans are not predisposed to make sacrifices, particularly in regards to their social welfare programs, or to increase their contributions to European conventional defense in order to create a more stable military environment on the continent.

This chapter examines West European nations' contributions to their own defense. It examines the financial costs of withdrawing American forces under a variety of scenarios. Additionally, it analyzes the strategic wisdom of withdrawing forces from Europe in the hope that we can reconfigure those forces to respond to contingencies outside of Europe. It accepts that there is a legitimate debate among informed defense analysts concerning whether or not Europeans could do more for their own conventional defense, if national decisions were made to shift resources from domestic economic to defense programs. At the same time, however, this chapter rejects the specious notion proposed by some analysts—e.g., Krauss—that there is not or should not be some cause and effect relationship between a country's overall economic growth and defense spending.[4]

## Europe's Military Contribution

Would we like to see Europeans do more for their own defense? Of course, we would. But in many respects this is the wrong question because the answer is obvious when asked in such a simplistic fashion. We would always like for someone to do more because that means we could do less.

The more appropriate question is: Are our European allies pursuing policies and strategies—even if they do not fully achieve them at all times—that are consistent with NATO's main goals? Those goals are deterring the Warsaw Pact from using military force to obtain its strategic objectives in Europe and maintaining a sufficiently robust peacetime military posture that the Warsaw Pact cannot clearly predict the outcome of an attack upon NATO. Despite understandable American desires to see Europeans do even more for their own defense, European persistence over the long term indicates a sense of resolve in the defense budget area that has not always been apparent in the United States.

Table 4.1 indicates that from 1971–1986 U.S. and non-U.S. NATO average annual increases in defense were not significantly different: 1.4

TABLE 4.1
## TOTAL NATO DEFENSE SPENDING
(CONSTANT 1986 DOLLARS IN BILLIONS - 1986 EXCHANGE RATES)

|  | 1971 | 1986 | TOTAL % CHANGE | AVERAGE ANNUAL% |
|---|---|---|---|---|
| BELGIUM | $ 2.20 | 3.40 | 55.1 % | 2.8 % |
| CANADA | 5.63 | 7.90 | 40.4 | 2.1 |
| DENMARK | 1.49 | 1.65 | 10.8 | .6 |
| FRANCE | 19.20 | 28.46 | 48.2 | 2.5 |
| GERMANY | 22.01 | 27.69 | 25.8 | 1.4 |
| GREECE | 1.17 | 2.42 | 106.5 | 4.6 |
| ITALY | 10.37 | 13.46 | 29.8 | 1.6 |
| LUXEMBOURG | .03 | .05 | 100.4 | 4.4 |
| NETHERLANDS | 4.32 | 5.32 | 23.2 | 1.3 |
| NORWAY | 1.50 | 2.17 | 44.7 | 2.3 |
| PORTUGAL | 1.25 | .94 | - 24.9 | - 1.4 |
| SPAIN | 3.96 | 6.01 | 51.8 | 2.6 |
| TURKEY | 1.09 | 2.77 | 153.1 | 5.9 |
| UK | 24.36 | 27.33 | 12.2 | .7 |
| US | 224.10 | 281.10 | 25.4 | 1.4 |
| TOTAL | 322.67 | 410.67 | 27.3 | 1.5 |
| NON-US NATO | 98.57 | 129.57 | 31.4 | 1.7 |

SOURCE:   DERIVED FROM DEPARTMENT OF DEFENSE, *REPORT ON ALLIED CONTRIBUTION TO THE COMMON DEFENSE*, A REPORT TO THE UNITED STATES CONGRESS (APRIL 1988), p. 88.

percent for the United States and 1.7 percent for non-U.S. NATO nations. That's the bad news and a typical example—along with Europeans' failure to meet the 1979 Long Term Defense Plan (LTDP) goal of a 3 percent annual real growth in NATO defense budgets—that NATO's critics often use to demonstrate Europeans' lack of commitment to their own defense.

On the other hand, the good news is that averaged out over the last 16 years only four countries—Denmark, Netherlands, Portugal and the United Kingdom—have failed to equal or exceed the United States in average annual defense budget growth measured in constant 1986 dollars. Also, as Figure 4.1 demonstrates, the European allies have adopted a slow but steady growth pattern, which is much more conducive to rational planning than the American "feast then famine" approach. From 1969–1977, real U.S. defense spending actually decreased by 30 percent. In an effort to make up for this deep trough in defense spending, U.S. defense budgets grew significantly during the early-to-mid 1980s—averaging between five to seven percent in real terms from 1981–1986. Not all of this real term growth, however, went into initiatives that directly applied to European defense. Offensive and defensive strategic nuclear programs consumed a significant portion of the DoD budget increases from FY 1981–1985. But, more importantly, the period of large increases in U.S. defense budgets has peaked and it appears that at best

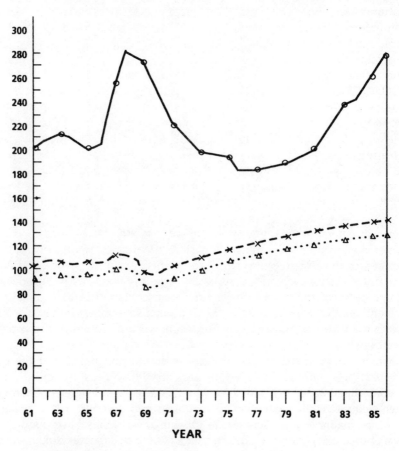

**FIGURE 4.1**
**TOTAL DEFENSE SPENDING (FISCAL YEAR)**
**U.S. DOLLARS IN BILLIONS**
**(1986 CONSTANT DOLLARS - 1986 EXCHANGE RATES**

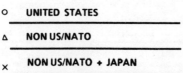

| o | UNITED STATES |
| Δ | NON US/NATO |
| × | NON US/NATO + JAPAN |

**BASED ON NATO DEFINITION OF DEFENSE SPENDING. EXCLUDES SPAIN.**

SOURCE:   DEPARTMENT OF DEFENSE, *REPORT ON ALLIED CONTRIBUTIONS TO THE COMMON DEFENSE,* A REPORT TO THE UNITED STATES CONGRESS, (APRIL 1988), p. 19.

U.S. defense budgets will keep pace with inflation. It is not improbable, however, that we will see a severe downturn in U.S. defense budgets, as was witnessed in the 1970s.

One can argue that Europeans may or may not have allocated the outputs from their slow but steady growth commitment in the most optimum fashion.[5] However, the steady persistence that the European community has demonstrated over the long run, particularly given the erratic nature of American defense budgets and the domestic economic problems that many Europeans had to face due to high U.S. inflation and interest rates in the 1970s, is very impressive.

*Quantifiable Factors.* As a result of this slow, but steady growth in European defense budgets, NATO major weapons inventories have been modernized and in some cases increased substantially. For example, between 1975 and 1987 European main battle tank holdings increased by approximately 35 percent, and infantry fighting vehicle holdings by 53 percent, with a major portion of those additions coming from British, Dutch and Belgian inventories. Also, the European allies bought about 1,000 front-line land-based aircraft and have ordered nearly another 900 planes to be delivered during the late 1980s or early 1990s.[6] In addition, European members of the Alliance deployed new anti-tank guided missile systems, expanded their attack helicopter inventories significantly, modernized their air defense systems, and bought a NATO AWACs system. Equally significant changes in European thought on doctrine and new operational concepts have developed over the last decade.

In terms of "outputs," then, the European record may not be perfect, but it is hardly fair to argue that they are seeking a "free ride" for their defense. If war should occur in Europe, NATO must be able to survive the first days and weeks of combat. The outcome of the early battles will in large measure be determined by the forces that are immediately available and in the theater. What is the European contribution to its own defense when one looks at the issue this way?

Based on International Institute for Strategic Studies figures, Europe's peacetime contribution to deterrence is not insignificant. For example, Europeans deploy 85 percent of the NATO divisions manned in peacetime—in the critical AFNORTH and AFCENT regions they field nearly 80 percent of the divisions.* Upon mobilization, European nations

---

*Allied Forces Central Europe (AFCENT) and Allied Forces Northern Europe (AFNORTH) are NATO operational commands. We are using the terms here to define geographic areas. Geographically, AFCENT includes all of the Federal Republic of Germany south of Schleswig-Holstein and NATO Europe north of Italy to the English Channel. AFNORTH, geographically, includes Denmark, Schleswig-Holstein, Norway, and the Baltic approaches to the North Sea.

will provide 80 percent of NATO's divisions and 65 percent of the divisions in AFNORTH and AFCENT. In peacetime, European-NATO nations contribute approximately 75 percent of the tanks; 90 percent of the artillery, multiple rocket launchers, and mortars; nearly 80 percent of the land combat aircraft; 70 percent of the armed helicopters; and 85 percent of the naval vessels in European waters for NATO's defense.

Since the majority of U.S. forces in peacetime are deployed in the Central Region, the European ratios of peacetime "outputs" for their own defense in AFNORTH and AFCENT are slightly less than for NATO as a whole, but they are still impressive. For example, European nations provide approximately 65 percent of the tanks; 80 percent of the artillery, multiple rocket launchers, and mortars; 80 percent of the land combat aircraft; 60 percent of the armed helicopters; and 80 percent of the ships that NATO deploys in AFNORTH and AFCENT in peacetime for deterrence and the immediate crisis period should deterrence fail.[7]

*Nonquantifiable Factors.* Items like tanks, infantry fighting vehicles, airplanes, artillery, and divisions are the easy indicators to demonstrate Europe's commitment to its own defense. In the long run, however, the non-quantifiable contributions may be more significant.

For example, how does one quantify the level of commitment to European defense that is demonstrated by numerous NATO countries bearing the burden of conscription; over 400,000 foreign troops on FRG soil and more than one million acres of West German land set aside for military installations and military use; by virtue of host nation support agreements, U.S. rent free access to bases and airfields throughout Europe; damage to territory, populations, and buildings as a result of over 5,000 annual military exercises in the FRG alone; and daily low-level military flights by NATO tactical aircraft?[8]

When NATO was once criticized for being too much of a burden for the United States to bear, Richard Burt, then Ambassador to the FRG, said: West Germany "is densely populated—60 million people and the size of Oregon. . . . I don't think most Americans would accept" the inconveniences that the FRG has been prepared to tolerate.[9] Obviously, one cannot prove Burt's assertion. But, through public pressure residents of Washington, D.C. and Northern Virginia were able to curb night time flights into National Airport because of noise pollution. If the Washingtonian and Northern Virginian response would be typical, one must wonder—as Burt said—how other Americans would react if they were confronted with what the average West German citizen must tolerate as part of his commitment to NATO: until 1988, at least 110,000 annual low level military aircraft flights, some of which occur at night.

Additionally, when it was not politically popular, NATO ultimately agreed to modernize its immediate range nuclear forces and to accept

U.S. controlled ground launched cruise missiles and Pershing IIs to be stationed on European soil. And NATO nations provide shelter for thousands of other nuclear warheads and dual capable systems, which make them obvious nuclear targets in the event deterrence fails.

Europeans, by virtue of their membership in NATO, provide the territory where the battles will be fought should deterrence fail. It is important to remember that we do not station forces in Europe for altruistic reasons. When forward defense is stripped of its political and diplomatic niceties, the bottom line is: if deterrence should fail, we would prefer to be in a position to fight on European—not North American—soil. Or, as John Maresca, a former deputy assistant secretary of defense for European and NATO policy, has said, "If your home were going to be attacked wouldn't you rather have the fight down the block rather than in your front yard."[10]

Finally, the standard indicators used in burdensharing debates (percentages of GNP or GDP spent on defense) skew the debates against Europeans. As a result, burdensharing critiques often do not give Europeans credit for hard-to-quantify contributions to European defense and deterrence. Over the years, DoD has been reluctant—and rightly so—to break out the defense budget and say "X" is spent on Europe, "Y" is spent on the Pacific, "Z" is spent on third world contingencies, etc. How and where we would deploy forces if deterrence should fail is situation dependent. Depending on how a crisis evolved, it is possible that the entire U.S. force structure, and as a result, the entire U.S defense budget could be devoted to European defense. On the other hand, depending on the circumstances and the specific crisis in question, forces might be deployed to several theaters. In other words, the budget allocations for those forces would, in theory, be parcelled to several theaters.

Under Congressional pressure in 1985, however, DoD did suggest that 60 percent of the defense budget related to European defense. On one hand, DoD's statement provided NATO's critics with additional fuel for their arguments that American defense budgets were bloated because of our European commitments. On the other hand, if one looks at the 60 percent figure from a burdensharing perspective, European contributions to Alliance collection defense do not look as bad as some analysts would have one believe and the American contribution to European defense may not be as out of proportion as some contend.

For example, if one uses 60 percent of DoD's budget as the benchmark for the American contribution to European burdensharing, the U.S. contribution to European defense is about 4 per cent of its GDP. This is only slightly higher than 3.3–3.5 percent that NATO-European countries have averaged since 1960. The 3 percent figure, however, does not take into account the social costs of conscription in many European countries, nor the fact that the FRG provides rent-free access to land and facilities used by U.S. and other allied forces or the West German economic support provided to Berlin. In fact, the Congressional Budget Office (CBO) has said that if one calculates these hidden costs into West Germany's burdensharing contribution the German share of its GDP devoted to defense would increase from 3.1 to 4.1 percent[11]—i.e., equal to the U.S. contribution, if one assumes that 60 percent of the U.S. defense budget is allocated to European defense programs.

Europeans' commitment to their own defense then is more than just weapons counts and dollars invested in defense—even though, as we saw earlier, Europe is not doing all that badly in these areas either. A balanced appraisal would have to conclude that Europe contributes a lot more in the hard-to-quantify areas than is always readily apparent. Also, in some instances, European contributions to burdensharing can be made to look good or bad depending on what one chooses to include as "hard data" initial inputs or assumptions.

## Costs and Risks

Two assumptions are always implicit to any argument that calls for the United States to alter its level of military commitment to Europe: (1) The U.S. will save money, free up forces for other contingencies, e.g. Southwest Asia or low-intensity conflicts, and any forces that might be withdrawn always could be redeployed to Europe in a crisis in any case; and (2) Europeans can and will pick up the U.S. slack. There is an endearing appeal to an argument which essentially says we can maintain our same intensity of interest in Europe—i.e., our basic goal to avoid a hostile nation or group of nations dominating the industrial potential of Europe does not have to be rejected. Moreover, we can achieve this goal with fewer forces in Europe because Europeans will have to do more, if we reduce our level of commitment. At the same time, we can build a flexible strategic reserve and do so at reduced costs because we will not have forces in Europe. One wishes strategy and security were so easy, but they are not.

*Financial Costs.* There is nothing new to the idea that we will save money if we pull forces out of Europe. Since the early 1970s, numerous studies have been undertaken to calculate the financial costs associated with withdrawing U.S. forces from Europe. Exactly how much a withdrawal will cost or save depends on assumptions used in regard to how much equipment will be prepositioned in Europe, how fast we want the forces to return to Europe, and availability of sea and airlift. Ultimately, however, the only way that one can insure that significant amounts of

TABLE 4.2
# U.S. TROOPS IN EUROPE: WITHDRAWAL COSTS AND SAVINGS
(IN MILLIONS OF DOLLARS)

| CALCULATIONS AND OPTIONS | ONE-TIME COST (+) OR SAVING (-) | ANNUAL COST (+) OR SAVING(-) |
|---|---|---|
| INITIAL CALCULATIONS | + 30 | |
| MOVEMENT TO UNITED STATES | | -45 |
| REDUCED NEED FOR CHANGE OF STATION MOVES | | |
| EMPLOYING U.S. INSTEAD OF FOREIGN CIVILIANS | | + 25 |
| REDUCED PIPELINE AND STORAGE COSTS | -30 | -20 |
| CLOSING FACILITIES IN EUROPE | + 10 | -5 |
| PROVIDING FACILITIES IN UNITED STATES | + 60 | + 5 |
|    NET COST OR SAVING | + 70 | -40 |
| | | |
| OPTION 1: ALL EQUIPMENT EXCEPT AIRCRAFT PREPOSITIONED IN EUROPE; NO ADDITIONAL AIRLIFT REQUIRED | | |
| MAINTENANCE COST FOR EQUIPMENT IN EUROPE | | + 40 |
| EQUIPMENT PURCHASED IN UNITED STATES TO REPLACE PREPOSITIONED EQUIPMENT IN EUROPE | + 300 | |
| | | |
| OPTION 2:  NO EQUIPMENT PREPOSITIONED IN EUROPE; ADDITIONAL AIRCRAFT REQUIRED | | |
| COST OF CAPACITY TO AIRLIFT DIVISION AND EQUIPMENT: | | |
|    BY M + 30 (24 C-5As) | + 600 | + 140 |
|    BY M + 15 (56 C-5As) | + 1,400 | + 340 |
| | | |
| OPTION 3:  NO EQUIPMENT PREPOSITIONED IN EUROPE: RETURNED BY M + 90 WITH EXISTING AIRLIFT AND SEALIFT | | |
|    NET COST OR SAVING | + 70 | -40 |

SOURCE: JOHN NEWHOUSE, U.S. TROOPS IN EUROPE; ISSUES, COSTS, AND CHOICES (WASHINGTON, D.C.; THE BROOKINGS INSTITUTION, 1971, P. 115. COPYRIGHT © 1971 BY THE BROOKINGS INSTITUTION. REPRODUCED BY PERMISSION OF THE PUBLISHER.

money are saved is to deactivate the forces that are withdrawn. Under any other set of circumstances, withdrawal is financially expensive and in some cases can cost the United States a *lot* of money.

For example, in 1972, the Brookings Institution examined three different options for withdrawing a division from Europe (see Table 4.2).[12] If the division's equipment remained in Europe and was prepositioned, Brookings estimated that the one-time cost (in 1972 dollars) to buy a set of equipment for the division that was restationed in the United States would be approximately $300 million. The study argued that it would cost $40 million annually to maintain the prepositioned set of divisional equipment in Europe.

The second option assumed that a division would be withdrawn and no equipment would be prepositioned in Europe. Brookings calculated that it would require a one-time cost of $1.4 billion to buy a sufficient number of aircraft to return the division and its equipment to Europe by M+15, and the annual operating costs for the additional airplanes would be $340 million. The one time costs could be lowered to $600 million and the annual operating costs to $140 million, if U.S. policymakers decided that they could tolerate the division not arriving in Europe until M+30.

Option three assumed that both men and equipment would be returned to the United States and no additional airlift or sealift would be procured. This clearly was the least expensive of the three options considered. The one-time costs would be low—on the order of $70 million—and Brookings calculated the annual operating savings for the division to be approximately $40 million. However, the division probably could not arrive in Europe until M+90. Based on this analysis the study concluded:

> The only way to effect large budget savings in military expenditures for NATO . . . is to deactivate troops assigned to NATO or oriented to meet European contingencies—whether they are stationed in Europe or in the United States. In other words, saving money depends not on reducing force levels in Europe but on reducing the total U.S. force structure.[13]

In 1982, responding to Congressional inquiries concerning the costs of U.S. deployments in Europe, DoD initiated a study to determine the financial costs or savings associated with withdrawing one division and one air wing or one Corps and two air wings from Europe under a variety of scenarios: POMCUS (Prepositioning of Material Configured in Unit Sets) vs. no POMCUS; forces remain in active force structure vs. reserves; additional airlift vs. sealift or no additional lift; and M+10 vs. M+30, M+40/70, or M+50/80 (see Figure 4.2).[14] According to DoD's calculations, it would cost $9 billion (in 1983 dollars) over a five year period to buy the necessary equipment to preposition a division and one air wing and the additional airlift to return those forces to Europe by M+10. The Corps and two air wing option was estimated to cost $19.2 billion over a five year period, if we wanted to meet our NATO M+10 commitments.

Costs could be reduced—but not eliminated—by dropping the POMCUS requirement and stretching out the time when forces were assumed to arrive in Europe. For example, DoD's analysis indicated that it would cost $2.5 billion to withdraw a division and one wing or $6 billion for a Corps and two air wings over a five year period. These figures were based on the following assumptions: the forces remained on active duty;

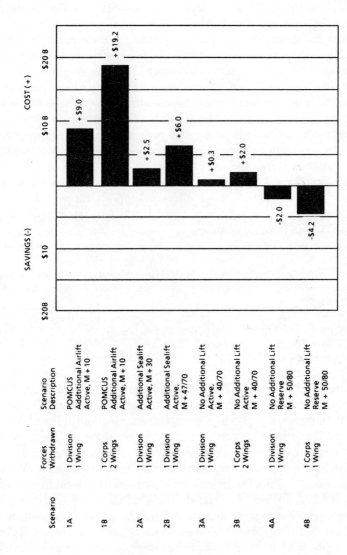

**FIGURE 4.2**
**SUMMARY OF FIVE YEAR (1984-88) SAVINGS/COSTS**
**(FYDP $ IN BILLIONS)**

| Scenario | Forces Withdrawn | Scenario Description | Savings/Costs |
|---|---|---|---|
| 1A | 1 Division 1 Wing | POMCUS Additional Airlift Active, M + 10 | + $9.0 |
| 1B | 1 Corps 2 Wings | POMCUS Additional Airlift Active, M + 10 | + $19.2 |
| 2A | 1 Division 1 Wing | Additional Sealift Active, M + 30 | + $2.5 |
| 2B | 1 Division 1 Wing | Additional Sealift Active, M + 47/70 | + $6.0 |
| 3A | 1 Division 1 Wing | No Additional Lift Active, M + 40/70 | + $0.3 |
| 3B | 1 Corps 2 Wings | No Additional Lift Active M + 40/70 | + $2.0 |
| 4A | 1 Division 1 Wing | No Additional Lift Reserve M + 50/80 | -$2.0 |
| 4B | 1 Corps 1 Wing | No Additional Lift Reserve M + 50/80 | -$4.2 |

Source: **Department of Defense.** *Report of the Secretary of Defense 1985 Authorization Request and FY 1984-1988 Defense Programs* (Washington, D.C.: U.S. Government Printing Office, 1983), p. 189.

their equipment was not prepositioned; and the United States would buy sealift to return the forces to Europe by M+30. If the U.S. bought no new strategic lift and did not preposition equipment, costs for a division and air wing or Corps and two air wing withdrawal would be $300 million and $2 billion respectively. In this scenario the forces would not arrive in Europe until M+40/70.

Like the earlier Brookings study, DoD's assessment concluded that the only way to save money from European troop withdrawals would be to deactivate any forces withdrawn, buy no extra strategic lift, and accept the fact that reinforcements for Europe in the event of a crisis or war would not arrive until much later (e.g. M+50/80). If one was willing to accept these conditions, a division and one air wing withdrawal could result in a $2 billion savings over a five year period, and a Corps and two air wing withdrawal could save the United States $4.2 billion over the same time period.

Finally, Table 4.3 indicates a 1987 CBO analysis of the costs and savings associated with three different options for withdrawing Army-only forces from Europe. Simply put, CBO's assessment confirms Brookings and DoD's earlier studies:

> All three approaches require a one-time investment to move withdrawn troops, perhaps with their equipment, back to the continental United States (CONUS). . . .
> Recurring savings would be large enough to offset these one-time costs rapidly *only if the troops that were withdrawn from Europe were also eliminated from the Army's endstrength.*[15]

*Political-Military Risks.* If the only way to save money is either to deactivate withdrawn forces or to put them in the reserves, then altering U.S. deployments in Europe must be examined in light of the political and military risks that the United States must be willing to accept. One of the most significant risks is that, if changes in U.S. forces occur unilaterally without major asymmetrical reductions in the Warsaw Pact threat brought about by conventional arms control, West European nations may not be capable of filling the U.S. military gap.

Despite what was said earlier concerning Europe's slow but steady commitment to its own defense, the past may not be prologue. Every indication is that it will be increasingly more difficult for European nations to expand their active force structures, given European financial and demographic trends.

The number of draft age males in Europe is declining significantly. In the case of the FRG, the number of males between 17–30 will drop

TABLE 4.3

## COSTS( + ) AND SAVINGS(-) OF WITHDRAWING TROOPS FROM EUROPE
### (IN MILLIONS OF FISCAL YEAR 1988 DOLLARS)

| | ONE-TIME COSTS | | | RECURRING ANNUAL SAVINGS |
|---|---|---|---|---|
| | EQUIPMENT | OPERATION & BASING SUPPORTa/ | TOTAL | OPERATION & SUPPORT a/ |
| **WITHDRAW 5,000** | | | | |
| MOVE TO CONUS; PREPOSITION EQUIP. | + 970 | 0 to + 140b/ | 0 | + 1,110 | -20 |
| MOVE TO CONUS; NO PREPOSITIONING | -- | 0 to + 140b/ | + 20 | + 160 | -30 |
| REDUCED STRENGTH | -- | -- | + 30 | + 30 | -230 |
| **WITHDRAW 20,000** | | | | |
| MOVE TO CONUS; PREPOSITION EQUIP. | + 2,910 | + 900 to + 970c/ | + 10 | + 3,890 | -100 |
| MOVE TO CONUS STET; NO PREPOSITIONING | -- | + 900 to + 970c/ | + 70 | + 1,040 | -110 |
| REDUCE STRENGTH | -- | -- | + 130 | + 130 | -920 |
| **WITHDRAW 100,000** | | | | |
| MOVE TO CONUS; PREPOSITION EQUIP. | + 6,320 | + 5,560 | + 70 | + 11,950 | -480 |
| MOVE TO CONUS; NO PREPOSITIONING | -- | 5,560d/ | + 360 | + 5,920 | -540 |
| REDUCE STRENGTH | -- | -- | + 670 | + 670 | -4,620 |

A.  NO ESTIMATES OF COSTS OR SAVINGS ARE AVAILABLE FOR RETURN OF FACILITIES TO GERMANY WITHOUT MORE DETAIL ON SPECIFIC WITHDRAWALS.

B.  THESE COSTS ASSUME THAT ALL EXISTING FACILITIES (INCLUDING TEMPORARY STRUCTURES) ARE USED TO STATION A BRIGADE-SIZE UNIT. THE ESTIMATE INCLUDE SOME ADDITIONAL NEW CONSTRUCTION, AND THE REHABILITATION OF TEMPORARY STRUCTURES.

C.  THE LOWER END OF THE RANGE ASSUMES THAT ALL EXISTING FACILITIES (INCLUDING TEMPORARY STRUCTURES) ARE USED TO STATION A BRIGADE-SIZE UNIT. THESE COSTS INCLUDE SOME ADDITIONAL NEW CONSTRUCTION, AND THE REHABILITATION OF TEMPORARY STRUCTURES. THE HIGHER END OF THE RANGE ASSUMES THE USE OF PERMANENT AND SEMIPERMANENT FACILITIES ONLY. THE ESTIMATES ASSUME THAT ADDITIONAL NEW CONSTRUCTION IS NEEDED TO STATION A DIVISION-SIZE UNIT.

D.  THESE BASING COSTS ASSUME CONSTRUCTION OF NEW FACILITIES FOR ALL WITHDRAWN TROOP. THUS, THEY PROBABLY REPRESENT AN UPPER BOUND ON COSTS. COSTS WOULD BE LOWER TO THE EXTENT THAT SPACE WAS AVAILABLE AT EXISTING FACILITIES.

SOURCE:  CONGRESSIONAL BUDGET OFFICE, "COSTS OF WITHDRAWING ARMY TROOPS FROM EUROPE", MEMORANDUM, MAY 8, 1987, p. 2.

by a total of two million between 1985 and 1999. A similar, but not so drastic, decline will occur in other Central Region states.[16]

Clearly there are alternatives for dealing with the European demographic trends. Nations could increase conscription periods, alter the male-female ratios, stretch-out the primary draft age period, etc. While there are options available, Americans should keep three basic points in mind. First, since the United States rejected conscription in the early 1970s as a social burden that was too much to bear, we are in a very poor position to try to tell our allies how they should alter their defense policies to maintain or increase their conscription options. Second, even if major alterations in European conscription policies were adopted, it still will be increasingly difficult for Central Region states to maintain current force levels with the projected decline in numbers of draft age males. Third, if Central Region states are able to maintain current active force levels, this should be viewed as a major indicator of their commitment to their own defense, given the political, social, and economic costs that they will have to bear to achieve this goal.

Also, Europeans may not be able to fill the U.S. military gap because of economics. If the United States were to withdraw, say 100,000 forces, our European allies would have to increase their defense spending by 18 to 30 percent over a two year period if there were a desire to offset the American reduction quickly. Such increases for defense are unlikely in the immediate future in any West European nation.[17]

Additionally, if the United States were to decide to withdraw substantial forces from Europe prior to a CFE agreement, we must accept the possibility that not only Europeans but also other allies might interpret our actions as a general retrenchment in U.S. overseas commitments and react accordingly. No matter how hard U.S. decisionmakers work to try and convince allies that this is not the case, it will be difficult to convince them otherwise. U.S. strategy and defense policy for the last 40 years has been anchored in Europe and forward defense. Implicitly—if not explicitly—withdrawing forces would have to be viewed as a fundamental change in U.S. policy and a lessening of commitment toward traditional allies. If withdrawn forces could not be maintained in the active force structure, the argument that we could react quickly to protect our allies and our interests would even ring more hollow.

Finally, it is hard to imagine how Saudi Arabia, Japan, Israel, Korea, and other important allies would be reassured that a reduced U.S. military presence in Europe would enhance the U.S. commitment toward them. If Americans were not willing to bear the cost and risks to remain in Europe, why should other nations expect that the United States would not apply the same logic to them since their historical, cultural, financial and military ties with the United States have never been as significant as Europe's.

*Disruptive European Nationalism.* Another risk is that U.S. actions could precipitate disruptive European nationalist tendencies. Those who favor Europeanization of Europe's defense (e.g., Helmut Schmidt, Sir Geoffrey Howe, Henry Kissinger, and David Calleo, to name just a few) essentially argue that overreliance upon the United States breeds contempt and resentment on both sides of the Atlantic and that all parties would be better off if Europeans strengthened their role in NATO. To a point, those who make this argument are correct. Recent German and French collaborative military efforts in the Central Region are positive steps to enhance NATO's conventional defense and similar future low-key initiatives should be encouraged, even if they do not result in France returning to NATO's integrated military command. But, if arguments for greater European involvement in its own defense are pushed to their logical conclusion and major U.S. troop withdrawals occur, it is not obvious that European stability is the only possible or even most probable outcome.

What would a reduced U.S. presence, with the possibility of further withdrawals if Europeans failed to plug the U.S. conventional holes, mean for Europe's nuclear guarantee? Some Germans already question U.S. resolve to use its nuclear weapons and to link American survival with German survival. A reduced U.S. presence and a less robust French and British guarantee are not likely to make Germans feel more secure. More importantly, while Paris and London may be discussing how to coordinate nuclear force plans with Bonn, neither country seems inclined to share control over their nuclear assets or the decisionmaking process for employing them in war. For example, France has refused to discuss the targeting issue directly. It has agreed to establish military-to-military discussions on nuclear questions, to establish a Paris-Bonn hot line and to give Bonn prior notice of any French decision to fire nuclear weapons on German soil. However, this is about as far as France is prepared to go at this time. Any German effort to create its own nuclear force will meet serious opposition in Eastern and Western Europe. A FRG intent upon arming itself with nuclear weapons is one of only two or three plausible scenarios that I can imagine that could compel the Warsaw Pact to attack NATO. Finally, does anyone believe that the French or British would offer to extend their nuclear guarantee to Norway, Turkey, or Greece?

Who would lead the Alliance, if the natural result of a smaller U.S. military presence were a reduced American leadership role in European affairs? Germany has the strongest economy and most capable conventional military forces. France and Great Britain are the only West European nuclear powers but neither one's conventional capabilities or economic power is equal to West Germany's. Despite recent cooperative military efforts between Bonn and Paris—which may be more the result of French concerns about FRG neutralist tendencies than real defense cooperation[18]—there are few political indications to warrant a conclusion that either country is willing to subjugate its national interests to create a United States of Europe. In fact, the opposite is the case: the FRG continues to believe that detente and Ostpolitik serve its national interests and are working toward these goals, despite normal and to be expected problems of execution. France, on the other hand, is less optimistic— as is the current Margaret Thatcher government—and more concerned about the Soviet threat than detente.[19]

The norm in European history is instability and military conflict. In part, this is the plight of continental powers whose territorial integrity and survival—the latter unlike the United States—can be threatened by conventional incursions from a stronger neighbor or group of neighbors. As a result, throughout European history there has been the constant search by individual actors for security. But, the problem from a continental power's perspective is that "if I am secure someone else has to be less secure."

A common threat in 1949 was a major cause for the Alliance's creation. However, what was and still is unique about the Alliance is the political underpinning of the U.S. commitment. In effect, what the United States told West Europeans when it agreed to commit American troops to the defense of Europe was: America will help balance Soviet power, as well as the specter of future German power, and, at same time, attempt to ameliorate one of the traditional causes of European political and military instability—namely the constant unilateral search for security by individual European actors. Specifically, from 1949–1951, this meant reassuring France, Great Britain, and the low land countries that the United States would over come its historical reluctance to become permanently involved in formal alliances to maintain the European balance of power. As one scholar has said:

> in order to reconstitute a balance of power against the Soviet Union, the United States had to become a part of a more intricate balance designed both to contain the Soviet threat and permanently end the threat of German domination of western Europe by integrating the western portion of that divided country into a larger Atlantic framework.[20]

Even if it were possible, as some observers contend, for West Europeans to provide the financial wherewithal for their own defense, the United States would want to remain within NATO as an active participant, more than likely with troops on the ground, because the United States is the only actor within the Alliance that does not and is not perceived to have any historical territorial designs on another country. As Josef Joffe said several years ago, the United States is Europe's "pacifier" and provides a glue to the continent that Europeans themselves have never been able to develop on their own.[21]

In other words, the political rationale for the U.S. commitment to Europe still remains as valid today as it was 40 years ago. A substantial change in the U.S. military role and participation in NATO, if it resulted in a concomitant loss of American political influence in the Alliance, would leave the FRG as the major economic and conventional military power actor in Western Europe. Lacking nuclear weapons, however, the FRG would still be vulnerable militarily. In a search to bolster its security, the FRG could spark classic European political maneuvering that in the past has led to instability and conflict.

The Alliance also is more than the Central Region of Western Europe. Who would provide the nuclear guarantee to Norway and Turkey should the United States fundamentally alter the character of its political and military commitment to NATO? The flank countries generally have no confidence that Britain or France would perform this important function. Also, they are not confident that the Central Region powers have the capability or will to reinforce them with conventional power in the event of a crisis or war.

Flank countries understand that NATO's Central Region powers are first continental powers, concerned primarily with their own interests, security, survival, and protection of territorial integrity. As a result, one is hard pressed to find support within the flanks for a fundamental redefinition of European security that would shift responsibility for their reinforcement to their Central Region partners. The flanks are just not confident that such unselfish actions would be exhibited by their European partners. Historically, it has not happened. When they asked themselves what has changed politically, economically, and militarily in Europe to make them believe that it would occur in the future, the answer that they generally give is nothing.

So what does this all mean? It means that there is tension within the Alliance because of American dominance for the first 30–40 years of NATO's existence. But, it does not mean that most Europeans want the United States to withdraw large segments of its forces from European territory. Nor, does it mean that large segments of the American population favor altering the U.S. security guarantee with Europe.[22]

Informed Europeans recognize that a withdrawal of American forces could feed the worst tendencies within a reinforcing power like the United States: i.e., the tendency to hesitate in crisis and not reinforce.

The tendency to say "let's wait and see what happens before we become engaged." The tendency to feed historical isolationist attitudes within American culture which are no longer appropriate for the economically, politically, and militarily interdependent world in which we currently live.

Also, many informed Europeans recognize that a substantial change in the political and military character of the U.S. military commitment to Europe has potentially adverse implications for the U.S. nuclear guarantee and ultimate political dominance within the Alliance. If the U.S. were to withdraw a larger number of forces from Europe, the most likely candidate to dominate the Alliance politically is the FRG and for many Europeans that is not a positive outcome. The bottom line then is: tension exists, but that tension in many European, as well as American, minds must be balanced with concrete realities. Those realities are that the "German issue" still remains; who can and would supply Europe's nuclear guarantee in the event of a U.S. withdrawal; and where would the flanks fit into a new European construct if the United States decided to play a less prominent day-to-day role on the European continent? These are largely political—not military—issues and our responses to them should be shaped with larger geopolitical and risk considerations in mind.


## Arms Control

Altering the U.S. role in NATO also could have adverse implications for conventional arms control. At the moment, NATO and the Warsaw Pact are involved in complicated and delicate discussions involving conventional arms control in Europe. Nothing formal has been agreed to, but in the wake of Soviet and East European unilateral reduction offers, NATO will more than likely face growing international political pressures—and domestic pressures as well—to move rapidly on reducing offensively oriented conventional forces from the Atlantic to the Urals.

The prospects for success in this arena are problematic. Given Soviet reinforcement capabilities, studies by RAND and others have indicated that NATO would have to obtain massive asymmetrical cuts on the part of the Warsaw Pact (e.g., on the order of 5:1 in tanks, artillery, and divisions) before any conventional arms control agreement would be in NATO's interest militarily.[23] Recent CFE proposals tabled by both the U.S. and USSR lean in the direction of major asymmetrical reductions in Warsaw Pact ground forces. However, other significant issues—e.g., should naval forces be included in the negotiations—still remain unresolved.

During the CFE negotiations it is quite likely that the USSR will continue to make gestures that are politically appealing, but not necessarily militarily significant to show its "good will" and "future" intentions to negotiate the withdrawal of even more forces. Both the United States and its Alliance partners must avoid becoming caught up in such diplomatic gambits. Unilateral Alliance reductions, for the appearance of "doing something in response to Gorbachev," could result in a NATO–Warsaw Pact conventional balance that is worse than it is now.

Therefore, threats or wide-scale public discussions that the United States might unilaterally withdraw forces from Europe or is considering significant changes in the American component of the trans-Atlantic bargain can only complicate the CFE negotiations. If the Soviets come to the conclusion that the United States might withdraw forces outside an arms control agreement, their incentives for negotiations could be reduced. Even if the current Soviet interest in conventional arms control is driven by a desire to lessen its military burden as a means to fix domestic economic problems, unilateral U.S. withdrawals—from a Soviet perspective—might still be preferable to a negotiated settlement.

The Soviets must realize that any major U.S. unilateral withdrawal would likely occur in the context of some political rift with Europe— e.g., disputes over burdensharing, out-of-area problems, differences over nuclear modernization, etc. In the aftermath of such a rift, Moscow could reap significant political and military benefits by offering to act as a responsible member of the European community and lead a European based initiative to reduce conventional forces.

Politically, a Soviet-led conventional arms control regime could result in further dividing Europeans from the United States and fuel European neutralist tendencies. Many Europeans and Americans already hold differing views on the nature of the Soviet threat. Moscow could profit politically by leading an arms control regime that played on these different views.

Militarily, if a significant withdrawal of U.S. forces preceded a conventional arms control agreement, the Warsaw Pact could agree to large asymmetrical cuts without significantly altering the military situation in Europe. In other words, unilateral U.S. withdrawals could allow Moscow to make massive cuts in its conventional forces, thereby helping Gorbachev to achieve some of his economic goals, but still leave the USSR as the dominant military power in the region—the worst of all possible alternatives.

On the other hand, if the United States and the Europeans can manage the CFE negotiations and obtain significant asymmetrical cuts on the part of the Warsaw Pact, while at the same time retaining the

U.S. nuclear guarantee intact, the end result could be not only a more secure Europe but also a more confident NATO. As part of a successful conventional arms control agreement, it is possible to envision a NATO that would feel reassured that neither American interests in nor commitment to Europe has lessened because the reduced U.S. presence occurred as a result of *Alliance-agreed-to negotiations* which achieved European stability at reduced levels of conventional forces.

Suffice it to say, threats of unilateral withdrawals in a post-INF environment, while conventional arms control negotiations are being considered, would be not only bad politics but also bad strategy. When it appears that Moscow, for the first time since the end of World War II, might be seriously thinking about sitting down with NATO to discuss possible conventional arms reduction alternatives, to give up 5,000, 10,000, or 100,000 U.S. troops in Europe without obtaining something directly in return—hopefully large, asymmetrical cuts in conventional forces by the Warsaw Pact—would not make much strategic sense.

## Force Structure

What impact would reducing U.S. military presence in Europe—either unilaterally or through arms control—have on U.S. military force structure? As we said earlier, the idea that withdrawing forces from Europe might result in more flexible forces that could be redeployed to Europe rapidly in a crisis and allow the United States to react more quickly to events in the Third World and Southwest Asia is appealing, but unlikely because the only way to save money is to deactivate the withdrawn forces. However, for the moment, let's assume that any forces unilaterally withdrawn or negotiated out of Europe were not lost to the active force structure and they were reconfigured for low intensity conflicts. If this occurred, lift requirements for these forces might be reduced and, as a result, it would be theoretically possible to return forces to Europe rapidly. The problem is that they would be the wrong types of forces needed for mid-to-high intensity armor mobile warfare in Europe where the risk of nuclear escalation would be ever present.

They also may be the wrong types of forces for even many Third World conflicts. Many Third World contingencies are not low intensity conflicts, as the recent Iran-Iraq War vividly demonstrated. The proliferation of highly accurate, cheap weapons in the Third World and the armor orientation of even second rate powers like Syria, Libya, and Cuba suggest that too light an expeditionary force might have survivability problems, even in Third World conflicts.[24]

Being able to arrive at a potential battle area rapidly prior to conflict is important for deterrence. Ultimately, however, to pose a credible threat that bolsters, rather than weakens deterrence, requires that forces deployed to a crisis area be capable of reacting to the threat that they might confront should deterrence fail. In Europe, this means maneuver warfare against an adversary who intends to try to crush NATO's forward deployed forces rapidly with armored and mechanized thrusts across the entire front. Units and forces organized for low intensity conflict lack the mobility and firepower to react to such a threat and should not be expected to do so.

Does the United States need more light-type forces for low intensity conflicts? U.S. ground forces are fairly light already. The total active and reserve Army and Marine Corps force structure is 32 divisions. Fifteen of those divisions could be considered "light," depending on one's definition of light, and available for use in Third World contingencies.[25] The main strategic problem, however, is that we lack enough strategic light to move even the current number of light divisions rapidly. Thus, creating more light or rapidly deployable divisions is not necessarily an answer but in reality would be a continuation of a basic strategic problem that we have refused to face for several years: inadequate strategic lift.

Additionally, we should ask ourselves if more "conventional-type, expeditionary" forces are the best instruments for dealing with most Third World conflicts. Clearly the term "Third World conflicts" is vague and imprecise and often has been used to cover anything from terrorism and narco-traffickteering to the Iran-Iraq war. Nevertheless, in a resource constrained environment the policy question is: should U.S. policy be focused on creating the military capabilities for expeditionary intervention in the Third World? Or, when possible, should we be attempting to use security assistance, intelligence gathering and sharing, civic action, humanitarian assistance, and show of force—when necessary—to support friendly nations? In other words, do what the United States can do best: assist, advise, economically and financially support, but avoid direct military intervention, except in instances like Grenada 1985 and Libya 1986, where our military activities were specifically focused and objectives and duration of engagement severely constrained.

Also, one should not assume—as Jeffrey Record has—that a readjustment in U.S. forces in Europe would affect only Army and Air Force units.[26] If part of the objective of altering the U.S. force deployments in Europe would be to save money, it would not be hard to imagine critics of a 15 carrier battlegroup/600 ship navy arguing that corresponding reductions in U.S. naval forces should occur, particularly if one tried to justify maintaining a large navy in order to ensure that oil flowed to Europe and Japan so our allies could remain afloat economically. Retiring two or three carriers and not commissioning replacements of associated support ships could save billions of dollars.

## Conclusion

Will all or any of these negative factors come to fruition? No one knows. It should be clear, however, that there are a significant number of political and military risks associated with reducing U.S. presence in Europe whether it is carried out unilaterally or through negotiations. The merits of any proposals should be evaluated carefully and the implications understood completely before they are adopted.

Europeans do not spend as much per capita on defense as does the United States. Most defense analysts would prefer that they spend more and believe that this is possible. However, as this chapter indicates, the contributions of West Europeans to their own defense are not insignificant. Also, in some instances, the indices used to evaluate relative burden-sharing do not completely or accurately represent European contributions. Over the long-term, our European allies have demonstrated the commitment to maintain a steady, predictable pattern of defense spending. The outputs from that commitment contribute significantly to the collective defense of Western Europe. Unfortunately, too many American defense analysts do not give the European allies the credit that they are due.

Clearly, all the allies—the United States included—could do more for conventional defense of Europe. A first step, however, must begin with the recognition that charges of "freeriding" inaccurately skew the debate. A second step must be the acceptance of the fact that NATO—and the West European states that form the Alliance—is fundamentally a regionally focused alliance and that the United States, on the other hand, is a global power. For the foreseeable future, the individual U.S. contribution to NATO will most likely be greater than any one West European nation's contribution. Such "burdens," however, are the realities of life for a global power that still requires the assistance of regional oriented states to achieve its global interests and objectives. A third step must be a recognition that withdrawing forces will not necessarily save the United States money and that maintaining a forward deterrent is not as financially expensive as some analysts would like us to believe.

# 5

# Policy Initiatives for NATO in the Future

As we look toward NATO's fifth decade, it is clear that the Alliance faces numerous challenges and opportunities. Many of those challenges will not be new or unique, as was discussed in previous chapters. Nevertheless, how the United States and the Alliance, as an entity, reacts to them could have a dramatic impact on West European security and global stability.

The North Atlantic Assembly, the Atlantic Council and the Center for Strategic and International Studies have already published major special studies on NATO's future with the expressed desire of shaping NATO's long-range political and military agenda.[1] These studies, in many instances, cover the waterfront with recommendations ranging from the need for a new Harmel Report to enhanced Alliance armaments cooperation and new weapons technology initiatives. This chapter has a more modest approach, but one that is consistent with the discussion of policy and strategy that was made in Chapter 2: i.e., it focuses on policy initiatives for the Alliance to address since policy should dominate the strategy process and define the political context within which strategy, force development, and weapons acquisition decisions should be made. The detail or specific actions to carry out the policy initiatives are not addressed for one simple reason. The process of executing policy decisions is important; but that process is often long and complicated, requiring extensive negotiations and bartering within the Alliance framework to obtain a consensus that is politically achievable and financially affordable. However, before that process—which is more tactical in character—can occur, there must be some agreement on the basic policy issues or decisions that need to be made.

## Public Education

The first issue that must be addressed is public education—not propaganda—concerning the threat that NATO faces and the minimum essential requirements needed for NATO's defenses. Every NATO nation must face the fact that the Alliance has been so successful in its major goal—deterrence of war on the European continent—that a sense of complacency exists within their general populations: i.e., since there has been no war in Europe for over 40 years, why should Europeans worry so much about military defense?[2]

As was discussed in Chapter 2, the reality is that currently a significant military threat to Western Europe does exist. Soviet and East European offers to unilaterally cut forces may affect Warsaw Pact short-warning attack capabilities. However, they will not eliminate the military threat, given Soviet force generation capabilities, nor change fundamental geopolitical realities. The USSR casts a long political shadow over Western Europe and always will by virtue of the fact that it sits squarely in the center of the Eurasian continent. These messages, however, are not always clearly perceived.

The Alliance needs to adopt a regular and systematic public education or public diplomacy program—not the ad hoc system that currently exists—that spells out not only these geopolitical realities but also the nature of the military threat confronting NATO. Some of the mechanisms for this type of program already exist, but they have laid fallow, in some instances, due to internal bureaucratic politics within NATO headquarters. In 1982 and 1984, NATO published a useful unclassified study entitled *NATO and the Warsaw Pact: A Force Comparison.* In 1988, NATO published a smaller, more quantitative report to support preparations for the CFE negotiations.[3] A four year hiatus between publications, however, is too long. Largely in response to DoD's *Soviet Military Power*, the USSR now annually publishes its view of the global "threat," which includes a major section on the NATO–Warsaw Pact balance.[4] NATO should also produce its own similar report annually or at least biennially.

Obviously NATO—as does each individual member state—produces numerous classified balance assessments. Also, there are highly regarded annual balance assessments like the International Institute for Strategic Studies' *Military Balance* in existence. But, without an official unclassified NATO publication, the Alliance is at some disadvantage in the public diplomacy debate.

It is essential that the NATO assessment be unclassified to be most useful. Those who see and use the classified studies already are aware and concerned that a threat exists. An unclassified NATO strategic military assessment produced on a regular schedule would be for public consumption. It would be a tool that journalists, academics, research centers, local opinion leaders, and the general public could use as they consider the issues relating to the European military balance. It is possible that such a publication would have no demonstrative affect on public opinion or even would have a negative effect, if West Europeans and Americans came to the conclusion that the military balance was not as bad as their governments claimed. The latter, however, is a risk that all democracies must be willing to take.

We must remember that NATO is involved in a long-term competition with the Soviet Union and the Warsaw Pact. To participate effectively in such a competition requires active public support. Without public support, which is based on information, there can be no consensus for the policies that governments want to pursue.

In addition, Moscow is already actively engaged in a public diplomacy campaign to affect West European perceptions of the conventional military balance. A broad-ranged Alliance effort to make unclassified information available to the public should be just one of several initiatives that NATO undertakes to undercut Soviet actions. Optimally, such an effort will create support for NATO's initiatives in conventional arms control, as well as informing the general public about the magnitude and complexity of the problem that the Alliance faces.

Individual West European nations, or NATO itself, also may want to consider an option that Great Britain adopted a few years ago. Recognizing a general lack of interest in the study of the history of war and the lack of financial capabilities within civilian institutions of higher learning to fund studies in military history, war studies, national security affairs, etc., the Ministry of Defense sponsored several positions in British colleges and universities in the general areas of national security affairs and war studies. NATO could do something similar in an effort to create a core group of educators who would teach and train Europe's next generation of leaders. The new European leadership generation will have no direct experience with war on the European continent. As a result, they will need a sound understanding of history, politico-military issues, and strategy to guide the Alliance as the pre–World War II generation passes from the leadership scene.

NATO should consider providing "seed" money to create two or three academic chairs in defense related studies in each of the Alliance countries over the next ten years. Each position should be funded for no longer than five years. After that time, the individual nation or university would be responsible for further funding of the positions. The total cost of such a program would be approximately $30–50 million over a ten year period—i.e. about the initial cost of one or two modern fighter aircraft. The costs of such a program would be a small price for NATO to pay in an attempt to create an environment to bolster public support for the Alliance during the first quarter of the twenty-first century.

## Nuclear Weapons

An integral part of any public education program should be to emphasize that, despite the zero-zero INF agreement and America's recent interests in a 50 percent reduction in strategic nuclear systems, nuclear weapons and nuclear modernization are still essential for NATO's defense and security. David M. Abshire, a former U.S. Ambassador to NATO, is correct when he says "the heart of deterrence in the 1990s will depend increasingly on NATO's conventional forces."[5] However, those who hope or wish for a nuclear free strategic environment are living in a fantasy world. The nuclear genie escaped from its bottle in 1945. There is no way to put it back, and, we probably do not really want to in any case. As Henry Kissinger and Cyrus Vance aptly pointed out in a recent issue of *Foreign Affairs*, fanciful and utopian claims of a completely denuclearized Europe "undermine serious discussion of a common Atlantic strategy and stigmatize the very weapons on which a credible deterrence and effective defense must be based for the foreseeable future."[6]

Nuclear weapons provide a considerable degree of uncertainty to a potential aggressor's risk calculations. They make it exceedingly difficult for a potential aggressor to predict the outcomes and results of his actions. Since the inability to predict confidently the outcome of a series of ill-defined events is one of the basic tenets of deterrence, it would make little strategic sense to undermine deterrence in NATO by adopting a no first use of nuclear weapons policy or attempting, in the immediate future, to eliminate all nuclear weapons.[7] Besides, Europeans have very little confidence in the ability of a totally non-nuclear environment to maintain deterrence. Rightly so, they point to numerous examples in history—many of which occurred on the European continent—to show how easily conventional deterrence has failed in the past.

Clearly, no one can empirically prove that nuclear weapons have caused deterrence to prevail in Europe for more than 40 years. Yet there has been no war in Europe during this time period, which is unique in European history. Even if it is true that in an era of nuclear parity the United States would have to consider more seriously whether or not it would actually fire its nuclear weapons to help defend its West European allies than it may have in an earlier age, this does not in and of itself invalidate the threat that they might be used. Ultimately, it is the *possibility* of nuclear use which bolsters European deterrence. As John Mearsheimer has argued:

> The deterrent value of a weapon is a function of the costs and risks of using that weapon as well as the probability that it will be used. Given

the consequences of using these horrible weapons, it is not necessary for the likelihood of use to be very high. It is only necessary for there to be a reasonable chance that they will be used.[8]

With more than 4,000 NATO nuclear weapons still deployed in Europe after the INF decision, plus the French and British independent strategic forces and the U.S. nuclear systems not dedicated to SACEUR, a "reasonable" chance continues to remain that nuclear weapons might be used should conventional deterrence fail. However, it will be imperative over the next several years that NATO continue to modernize its nuclear forces—particularly its shorter range missile systems to maintain the nuclear deterrent. The latter will not be an easy task, given the anti-nuclear sentiment existing in several European capitals. Nevertheless, a sufficiently robust and redundant NATO nuclear deterrent—within the guidelines and parameters of the INF and the Montebello Agreements—will be just as critical for European deterrence in the twenty-first century as it was for the latter half of the twentieth century.

The United States will need to work within the Alliance structure on this issue. Unilateral American initiatives like the 1970s enhanced radiation proposals are likely to fail and be politically divisive in a time when Alliance cohesion already is stressed. To be successful, nuclear modernization proposals will need to be perceived, and in fact need to be generated, predominately from within the European community. The U.S. may want to consider reducing its number of battlefield nuclear artillery—possibly on the order of 50 percent—in return for European support to modernize LANCE.

## NATO Strategy and Doctrine

In recent years, NATO's strategy and doctrine have come under criticism from a variety of quarters. One group of critics—supported by individuals like Egbert Boeker, Lutz Unterseher, Horst Altfeld, Jochen Loser, Albrech von Muller, and Andreas von Bulow, to name just a few—contend that, given new military technologies, NATO can adopt a non-provocative or defensive-defense strategy and doctrine.[9] While differences in methods and tactics exist, fundamentally proponents of the non-provocative or defensive-defense schools of thought are advocating modifications in NATO's strategy and doctrine toward more typical area defense and mobile defense concepts. Supporters of this view contend that NATO should eschew its investments in offensive strike forces (e.g., armored formations and longer range strike aircraft), toward lighter infantry forces, small mobile anti-tank guide weapons (ATGW) units, artillery, and smart mines. The basic concept would be to confront an attacker with a multi-layer defense of smaller, territorially oriented units that have highly accurate and lethal weapons which could harass, attack through hit-and-run tactics, and ultimately disrupt Soviet breakthrough timetables making it impossible for the Warsaw Pact to plan or execute a short war scenario in Europe.

Proponents contend that confronting the Warsaw Pact with such a possibility would enhance deterrence. Moreover, non-provocative defense advocates argue that fundamentally altering NATO's capabilities to initiate offensive actions against Warsaw Pact territory would bolster crisis stability. With NATO having a reduced offensive strike capability, it is assumed that there would be fewer incentives on the part of the Warsaw Pact—and none on NATO's part—to initiate preemptive attacks during a crisis when the "fog of war" and concerns about the other side's intentions would be the most pronounced.

The opposite extreme of the defensive-defense concepts—a conventional retaliatory strategy—was proposed by Samuel Huntington originally in 1982 and then refined in his subsequent writings.[10] Huntington essentially argued that a deterrence by denial strategy—e.g., non-provocative defense—was ineffective in the current age. To bolster deterrence, NATO had to have a strategy and doctrine that incorporated punishment as well as denial. Given nuclear parity, Huntington argued that punishment based on nuclear weapons was no longer credible. As a result, to restore the punishment component to NATO's strategy, Huntington advocated that the Alliance should alter its traditional strategy and acquire the conventional capabilities necessary to attack and temporarily hold major portions of East European territory in the event of a NATO–Warsaw Pact war.

We do not need to go into an indepth analysis of the non-provocative defense concepts or the conventional retaliatory strategy here, since others have done that rather well.[11] Suffice it to say, the major weakness of the non-provocative defense proposals is the problem inherent to all area or mobile defense schemes. Ultimately to be successful, they have to accept that space will be traded for time, as the defender attempts to wear down the aggressor. But, NATO has no space—particularly with France not part of NATO's integrated military command structure. And, any space that might be traded would belong to West Germany—one of the most critical linchpins for a cohesive NATO defense. As a result, such concepts—even if they contain some good ideas like greater use of mines, barriers, and "smart" sensors linked to "intelligent" weapons—are not politically acceptable to most West Germans.

The conventional retaliatory option also is politically unacceptable, but for different reasons. NATO's operational doctrine has always had an offensive component to it—whether that component was offensive counter air; air strikes on Warsaw Pact airfields, fixed installations, bridges, ammunition storage sites, transshipment points, etc.; or nuclear strikes in Eastern Europe and the Soviet Union. As a result, to some degree SACEUR's Follow-On Forces Attack (FOFA) concept and even the U.S. Army's AirLand Battle Doctrine were not new ideas when they were originally proposed. Huntington, however, suggested using NATO ground forces to seize and hold critical territory deep within Eastern Europe—e.g., Prague, Leipzig, and Dresden. Despite Huntington's claims to the contrary, this would be just too much offense for a defensive alliance like NATO to adopt.[12] More importantly, however, if NATO somehow could muster the political will to pay for the additional forces that would be required to execute a conventional retaliatory strategy, there would be little need to change NATO's current strategy. The additional forces would be sufficient to bolster not only NATO's defenses but also deterrence as well.[13]

The important point here is that, despite criticisms of NATO's strategy and doctrine, the concept of Flexible Response and defending as far forward as possible are still valid principles given the political realities within the Alliance. As was discussed in the previous section, if NATO continues to modernize its nuclear weapons in a post-INF environment, the ultimate punishment component of Flexible Response should continue to exist. Alliance members may continue to question whether the U.S. will use its nuclear weapons to defend West Europeans, but Kremlin decisionmakers cannot confidently predict that it will not—particularly as long as more than 350,000 soldiers and airmen are deployed in Europe.

Additionally, the idea of rejecting forward defense—whether it would be to adopt offensively oriented concepts or a more mobile area defense— is a political anathema to most Europeans. An offensively oriented alliance runs counter to the European view that a defensive alliance is what makes NATO politically strong and supportable within the European publics. Too much passive defense, on the other hand, is equally insupportable because it implies a willingness to sacrifice Germans for other Europeans. West Germany is critical to the defense of Europe's Center Region. Therefore, to most Europeans forward defense is a small price to pay to reassure the most front line state that every effort will be made *not* to sacrifice its territory and to insure that the FRG remains within the Alliance.

For these reasons alone, NATO should continue to emphasize, as it has at its recent ministerial meetings, that the Alliance has no intention of reviewing its basic strategy or establishing a group of "wise men" to develop a new Harmel Report for the 1990s. Rather the Alliance should formally and regularly develop the issue that the basics of the

1967 Harmel Report are still valid: (1) where appropriate, NATO will pursue measures to reduce East-West tensions; and (2) NATO intends to maintain a defense—both conventional and nuclear—sufficient to deter any Warsaw Pact aggression.

## Deep Attack Versus Initial Defense

NATO continues to waver between whether it should emphasize its initial defense capabilities or to place greater emphasis on high technology, deep-attack weapons systems. In 1985, the NATO defense ministers approved MC 299—the Conceptual Military Framework (CMF) for NATO Defense Long Term Planning. This document was intended to provide military guidance for NATO's long-term resource planning. If the unclassified reports are accurate it is unfortunate, however, that no sense of priorities among NATO's five key mission areas seems to have emerged from this document.[14] Rather, all key missions apparently were determined to be equally important:

> . . . at Alliance level it is neither correct nor logical to attempt any prioritisation of the KMCs [Key Mission Components]. MNCs [Major NATO Commands] may set priorities for their commands and it will remain the responsibility of each nation to determine its contribution to Allied defense—and that includes any priority which a nation may wish to establish for the provision of its assets to the MNCs.[15]

General Bernard Rogers, the former SACEUR, favored emphasizing NATO's deep-attack capabilities—FOFA—through the procurement of emerging technologies. The underlying rationale being that NATO commands should have the capability to withstand an attack from the initial Warsaw Pact divisions in the forward areas. However, successive waves of follow-on forces, it was assumed, would ultimately (in less than two weeks, General Rogers was fond of saying) wear down NATO's defenses and Soviet Operational Maneuver Groups (OMGs) would then penetrate NATO's defenses. To be successful, however, would require precise timing on the part of Warsaw Pact forces. They would have to stay dispersed in rear areas in order not to become lucrative nuclear targets. Then, breakthrough forces would have to arrive at the right time and place to exploit weaknesses in NATO lines that earlier deploying forces had caused and identified. With FOFA and new deep-attack conventional technologies, SHAPE believed that it could upset the Warsaw Pact's timetables, by destroying reinforcing units before they arrived in the forward areas. This was supposed to make it difficult—if not impossible—

for Moscow to insure that its OMGs would arrive in time to exploit breakthrough opportunities.

Reputable analysts of Soviet operational art and doctrine have argued, however, that this may have been the way that the Soviets intended to fight in the 1970s, but it does not represent Soviet doctrine and concepts for the future. For example, Christopher Donnelly, Phillip Petersen, John Hines, and David Greenwood maintain that the Soviets intend to commit multiple OMGs on the first or second day of conflict.[16] The goal will be to create several breakthroughs along NATO's front and effectively to preempt NATO from using nuclear weapons. Echelons, if they exist, will be blurred and clearly not distinctive enough to attack in the manner envisioned by FOFA.

If this view of Soviet operational art and doctrine is correct, then strong NATO initial forces will be critical to prevent early breakthroughs. Additionally, NATO will not have sufficient time to allow its operational reserve to be created from reinforcing American units. European reserves that can be rapidly mobilized and are capable of defeating relatively large armored Soviet formations in maneuver war will be essential for NATO's defense.

This is not the place to argue which concept is correct. It is important, however, for NATO on the political or policy level to decide which one of these threat scenarios deserves the most immediate attention. Given financial realities within NATO, it is unlikely that the Alliance has the ability simultaneously to fund the capabilities to counter each of these concepts. The CMF will be of little value since it does not establish priorities among NATO's five key mission areas. If the Alliance fails to establish some sense of priorities, however, it could very well dissipate scarce resources across each mission area, creating just enough capability in each to lose in everyone in the event of war. On the other hand, by prioritizing the mission areas, NATO will have a better chance of focusing resources in the most critical areas.

It is difficult for a single nation to prioritize resources among its competing military requirements. For an Alliance of 16 nations, the problem is 16 times harder. Nevertheless, if the goal of the CMF is to guide Alliance long term resource allocations, it is imperative for NATO to decide which of its mission areas deserve attention first, which ones second, and so on. To do otherwise is to continue the pattern that NATO has followed for the last 40 years. To some degree, that would not be all bad, given our discussion of West Europeans' contributions to their own defense in Chapter 4. However, since NATO already spends about the same amount on defense as does the Warsaw Pact but does not seem to obtain an equal output, most observers would agree that a more rational expenditure of funds within NATO could not but help

West European defense and deterrence. For NATO to decide if it were going to emphasize deep attack or initial defense and not be continually torn between the two concepts could be a start toward a more rational planning process.

## Territorial and Home Defense Forces

Alliances, like chess players, must have an endgame in mind, i.e., a plan for how to use all the available pieces at one's disposal in the most efficient manner to ensure victory. NATO currently lacks such an endgame because it is unable to base its plans on using all the assets that are available to each nation.

Major NATO Commanders can base their military plans only on those forces and resources that each Alliance member has agreed to allocate to NATO as a result of NATO's formal defense planning system. However, there are relatively large numbers of territorial defense forces or home defense units that exist within most European countries. Generally, these forces are not committed to NATO and cannot be used for planning purposes in the Alliance's forward defense. In some cases, these forces make up more than 50 percent of the total military forces available to a particular West European nation. There is too much available military potential within these forces not to integrate them into NATO's forward defense plans, given the scarcity of resources that NATO has for its defenses. NATO should actively pursue a program that would ultimately culminate in allowing NATO commands to equip, train, and, most importantly, *plan* for using the large number of home defense elements as part of NATO's forward defense.

Two of my colleagues at the Strategic Concepts Development Center have examined the issue of how to make more effective use of European territorial or reserve forces. Andrew Hamilton favors the creation of heavy reserve armored/mechanized divisions. Given the excess trained manpower existing in the Central Region nations as a result of conscription, Hamilton argues that NATO should be able to field an additional 20–45 Heavy Division Equivalents (HDEs) from the European reserve systems. The cost for 45 new HDEs would be $198 billion in 1984 dollars and would require approximately a 1.7 percent annual real increase over a 15-year period, according to his calculations. Twenty new HDEs could be fielded in 10 years with a real growth of 1.4 percent a year.[17]

Karl Lowe contends that Belgium, the Netherlands, West Germany, and the United Kingdom could add a total of 11 new divisions—primarily infantry—to NATO's forward defense forces, if those countries would reorganize and restructure their current forces.[18] Lowe's proposal would still leave a substantial pool of forces for home defense or rear area security missions: 2 airmobile divisions and 6 Jaegear regiments, in the case of West Germany; 2 brigades in the Netherlands; 1 brigade and 9 regiments in Belgium; and 6 brigades in the case of the United Kingdom. West European nations also would retain the option of creating additional reserve units for home defense by reorienting part of the large European trained manpower pool from individual unit replacements to organized units.

Some rear area security risks would have to be accepted under Lowe's proposal. However, each Central Region nation has significant numbers of border police or national police that could be assigned rear area security and point defense security missions in the event of war. Also, before one worries too much about rear area security, it is necessary to think through the relationship between forward defense and rear area security missions. Namely, if NATO's forward defenses fail due to an inadequate number of forces dedicated to that mission, even the current number of forces assigned to rear area security would be insufficient to deal with Soviet OMGs and regular Warsaw Pact forces engaged in breakthrough and exploitation operations. As a result, Lowe's proposal tilts in favor of enhancing forward defense under the assumption that a stronger forward defense capability, to some degree, would minimize rear area threats. It is not clear that the opposite would be true and that is why forward defense is emphasized, even at the expense of home defense missions.

As in the case of deep-attack versus forward defense, it is not necessary here to advocate whether these concepts should be implemented or to analyze the mechanics of their implementation. They do, however, point toward a major policy issue that NATO needs to address: Can the Alliance and major NATO Commanders afford to continue to plan on employing only those forces which formally have been committed to NATO? Or, should the Alliance take actions to integrate the substantial territorial and home defense forces into the NATO planning framework? The same set of questions apply equally to other resources available to the Alliance, but these resources are not considered within NATO's military planning because they are not controlled by Ministries of Defense: e.g., local police, border control forces, reserve stocks of POL, etc.[19]

## French LOC and Planning

Despite recent cooperative defense efforts between France and West Germany and the symbolic creation of a joint brigade, it is unlikely that Paris at any time in the near future, will return to NATO's integrated command structure. Paris has moved toward a more flexible policy regarding its role in a NATO–Warsaw Pact war and both Giscard d'Estaing and Francois Mitterrand have—rhetorically at least—expressed greater support for the idea of early French participation in a European war. Nevertheless, officially France still subscribes to the policy that there will be no "automatic" commitment of French forces in a crisis or war.[20] More importantly, within French political circles, a rather strong consensus still seems to exist that Paris must continue to maintain its doctrinal flexibility because French self interests are best served with such a policy and because of lingering suspicions over American will in a crisis.

Even if France does not rejoin NATO's integrated command structure, enhanced French-NATO peacetime logistical planning could significantly enhance West European chances of surviving the early days and weeks of a war. A cohesive NATO defense is in French interests. Therefore, the idea of greater peacetime logistical planning between France and the Alliance should fall within the range of logical possibilities to pursue.

NATO's current logistical support infrastructure is fragile and vulnerable. Essentially NATO's Central Region logistical lines of communication (LOC) for reinforcements and resupplies—not arriving by air—flow through three major ports: Antwerp, Rotterdam and Bremerhaven. There are numerous alternative ports (e.g., Hamburg, Wilhelmshaven, Bremen, and Amsterdam), but the preferred planning ports are still Antwerp, Rotterdam, and Bremerhaven. More importantly, all of the Belgium, Dutch, and North German ports are in easy range of Soviet aircraft and are clustered essentially in a small geographic area. This simplifies the Warsaw Pact's targeting problem.[21] Access to French ports and logistical system would not only complicate Soviet planning but also provide NATO with much needed redundancy.

Given France's desires to maintain its separate identity as well as "*being seen* by all to be maintaining her independence," it is not likely that Paris will formally commit her ports and logistical system to NATO prior to conflict.[22] As a result, most assessments conclude that it would take "weeks, perhaps months," before a NATO-French LOC could be established.[23] That is too long; it should be possible to shorten the transition time, if some indepth prewar planning and coordination occurred.

NATO and individual members of the Alliance—particularly the off shore reinforcing members like the United States, Great Britain, and Canada—should seek ways to shorten the amount of time that it would take to open the French LOCs. For domestic political reasons, Paris will have to avoid any implication that it intends "automatically" to open its ports, railroads, airfields, road networks, etc. to NATO. However, peacetime planning against theoretical contingencies—which is the heart and soul of all military operational planning—should be possible. Such planning would help clarify several important issues: What is the through put port capacity of French ports; which French airfields could be made available to NATO in the event of a war; will there be any excess French railroad capacity after taking into consideration French military and domestic requirements; and how do the French intend to use their road network?

As David Yost, Stephen Flanagan, and others have suggested, the optimum solution would be for NATO and France in peacetime to initiate the necessary actions that would allow testing the French logistical networks, and actually readying Alliance supplies to stockpile when the French LOC becomes available.[24] If the optimum solution proves unachievable, however, NATO and individual member states should pursue the more modest goal outlined here: enhanced staff peacetime planning and coordination as a first step. This has a better chance of being politically acceptable in Paris at this time. If successful, more grandiose options could evolve over time.

## The United States Is a European Power

Walter Lippmann once wrote:

> . . . the behavior of nations over a long period of time is the most reliable, though not the only index of their national interests. For though their interests are not eternal, they are remarkably persistent. We can most nearly judge what a nation will probably want by seeking what over a fairly long period of time it has wanted; we can most nearly predict what it will do by knowing what it has usually done. We can best separate appearance from the reality, the transient from the permanent, the significant from the episodic, by looking backward whenever we look forward. There is no great mystery why this should be: the facts of geography are permanent . . . thus successive generations of men tend to face the same recurrent problems and to react to them in more or less habitual ways. Even when they adapt themselves to a new situation, their new behavior is likely to be a modification rather than a transformation of their old behavior.[25]

Lippmann's observation is particularly applicable to U.S. national policy and strategy. Early in its tenure, the Bush Administration should take every opportunity to reconfirm the importance of historical geostrategic realities in U.S. national security planning, as Lippmann suggested nearly 50 years ago. One of the first tasks of the new Bush Administration will be to define the direction and scope of American national security policy for the next four to eight years. As has become common practice, this will more than likely mean commissioning the National Security Council staff to write a national security directive (e.g. a NSC-68, PRM-

10, or NSDD-32 type document) that outlines the administration's goals, policies, and regional priorities. The administration already has begun this process through the initiation of a series of national strategy reviews on topics ranging from arms control policy to regional policy initiatives. At the same time that this process is underway, there should exist a number of opportunities for the administration to emphasize the importance of Europe in the U.S. national security planning process. The administration should use these opportunities to reconfirm unequivocally that the United States sees itself as a European power, does not intend to unilaterally withdraw forces from Europe, and continues to believe that Western Europe will be the most important overseas region of importance in U.S. defense planning for the foreseeable future.

Such definitive statements by the president and other senior representatives would do several things. First, for the immediate future, it would put to rest European concerns relating to the various proposals advocating a unilateral withdrawal of American forces and be a clear statement that such proposals do not reflect U.S. policy. Second, it would lend support to Alliance negotiations for conventional arms control. The Soviets would be put on notice that they could not expect to divide the Alliance through traditional salami tactics. If the Warsaw Pact wants a conventional arms reduction agreement, from an American perspective at least, it will have to occur as a result of alliance to alliance negotiations. Third, it will begin the process to establish a clear set of priorities for various departments and agencies to use in their planning. Obviously, it will be necessary to articulate the relative importance of other regions of the world. That will not be an easy task. Nevertheless, the process must be started. It would be better to begin early and not allow the process to drag out as initially occurred in the Reagan Administration.

To sum up: There are several major policy initiatives that remain unresolved within the NATO alliance. It is feasible that the traditional approach of "muddling through" would be sufficient to maintain deterrence on the European continent. However, given the fact that a new American president took office in 1989 and the administration has initiated a major strategy review, opportunities should exist to address the issue of why Europe continues to be important to the United States. Neither the United States nor the Alliance should eschew these opportunities. But even more importantly, it is the type of policy issues that have been addressed in this chapter that need to be approached first before we move down the path of irreversibly implementing more tactical issues such as enhanced armaments cooperation, burdensharing, and the types of airplanes and tanks that nations should buy for the twenty-first century. Policy should drive strategy, force development decisions, and tactics not vice versa.

# 6

# Summary

This effort to examine the strategic importance of Western Europe to the United States is by its very nature an incomplete strategic assessment. If, however, this assessment leads even just a few American policymakers and analysts to eschew ideas that somehow the United States would be better off, obtain greater strategic flexibility, or reduce its financial defense burdens if it would alter its strategic relationship with NATO, this study will have served one of its purposes.

As was discussed in Chapter 1, NATO's critics are a disparate group. While there is no agreement among the critics on all the issues, there are common threads running through the basic argument that, given the current strategic environment, the United States needs to initiate an fundamental reevaluation of the American role in Europe in order to match ends with means. Four of those threads are: First, Western Europe is not as strategically important to the United States as it once was. Given new economic realities, particularly the growing economic importance of the Far East, the United States needs to readjust its regional priorities and force deployments to reflect a fundamental shift in the world's economic center of gravity. Second, West Europeans have historically refused to pay their fair share of their defense burden. Threatening or, in fact, withdrawing substantial forces from Europe will force Europeans to assume a more equitable share of their defense burden. Third, U.S. domestic economic realities will leave American policymakers with few options. Therefore, some advocates essentially argue that we should take this "forced" opportunity to reduce American dominance of the Alliance, which in the long run is an unhealthy relationship for both Americans and Europeans, and strive to create a stronger European pillar. This is supposed to result inevitably in a more enduring relationship with NATO and a stronger Alliance. Fourth, by withdrawing a substantial number of U.S. forces from Europe, the United States will save money and be able to restructure forces for more likely future military conflicts in the Third World.

The basic thrust of this book has been that each of these arguments is flawed. This does not mean that in some instances the goals, for example the desire to see a stronger more viable European component of NATO's defenses, are wrong. Quite the contrary is true. Rather, the means that are advocated seem unlikely to achieve the desired results.

In other instances, however, the basic assumptions are faulty. Trade alone does not define why a particular region of the world is important to the United States. A more complete assessment of the full panolpy of economic, geopolitical, and sociological indicators suggests that Western Europe will continue to be the prize in Soviet-American competition for the foreseeable future. The post–World War II economic boom that has occurred in the Far East may have altered the strategic environment. However, trends do not indicate that the world's strategic center of gravity has dramatically shifted. Also, Western Europe is militarily threatened and will probably continue to be threatened, even after a CFE agreement, in ways like no other region of the world.

Observers would prefer that NATO spend more for its own defense. But, that desire must be tempered with the realization that West Europeans, in a rather predictable fashion, have followed a pattern of slow, but steady defense growth over the last 15 to 20 years whereas the American approach has been one of cyclical feast, then famine. The outputs of this European approach are not insignificant, as were developed in detail in Chapter 4. Additionally, assessments of the European contribution to their own defense should take into consideration several non-quantifiable factors that critics often overlook: rent free access to military facilities, the territory on which any war may be fought, peacetime manuver damage to European territory and property, and the dislocation caused in West Germany alone by having more than 400,000 foreign troops on its soil.

Withdrawing forces from Europe will not save money for the United States—in fact, in the short run it will cost money—unless we change our basic policy and strategy goals. Also, there are no guarantees that American forces withdrawn from Europe would be reconfigured for more likely conflicts in the Third World. If the primary motives for withdrawing American forces were desires to save money, then those forces would have to be lost to the active force structure before any long term savings could be realized. In either case, without a major reduction in the Soviet threat via arms control, whether the withdrawn forces were reconfigured for other contingencies or lost to the active force structure, the United States would have to accept a higher level of risk in Europe since it would have fewer forces that were capable of fighting the type of high intensity manuever warfare called for in the event of deterrence failure in Western Europe.

Finally, one of the possible outcomes of greater Europeanization of Europe's defense is a stronger Alliance. Other outcomes are also possible, however, and it is unfortunate that NATO's recent critics have not examined those options with the same fervor or detail as they have the European pillar concept. The Alliance stretches from Norway to Turkey. It is not a European Center Region alliance only. Which one of the Central Region European powers would be willing to guarantee Norway or Turkey's security if the Central Region were not directly threatened? Even in the Central Region, who would lead the Alliance if the natural consequences of more Europeanization of Europe's defense were a reduced American presence in Europe? Who would provide the nuclear guarantee for the entire Alliance? One cannot wish these tough questions away. They require careful analysis before taking actions that could result in undermining nearly 40 years of European stability—a characteristic that is unique in twentieth century European history.

Strategy is about making choices. Those choices can be made consciously or unconsciously, but they cannot be avoided, given resource constraints. This book has argued that, for a variety of reasons, the most rational choice for the United States is to continue to assign NATO-Europe as the highest priority overseas region in its national security planning framework.

But even after making this choice, the Alliance, as well as the United States, faces other important policy choices in the near future that require resolution. We discussed some of those choices in Chapter 5. However, it is necessary to underscore that strong American leadership will still be essential for the foreseeable future. Like it or not, NATO largely continues to be a group of regionally oriented nations that have banded together to form a regionally oriented alliance. As a result, according to Robert Komer, "our allies still at bottom rely on Washington to provide the lead."[1]

The American leadership style that is required is one that emphasizes consistency rather than incongruity; persuasion—as well as offers of concrete incentives—and inducements for our allies to take their own actions to enhance European defense and deterrence; and perseverance rather than vacillation. It should not be beyond the ability of the United States to provide such leadership.

Critics of NATO will probably contend that such an approach will reap few rewards and encourge West European "free-riding" tendencies. However, as was pointed out earlier, contributions of West Europeans to their own defense are not insignificant. If those outputs are what "free-riding" is all about, then let's stay on the train we have been riding for the last 40 years.

This does not mean, however, that we should be complacent about the military situation in Europe. Obviously, we need to improve NATO's efficiency. The Alliance spends nearly the same amount on defense as does the Warsaw Pact. However, NATO's GNP is nearly triple that of its adversary ($6.8 trillion versus $2.6 trillion). Western Europe alone has a population base larger than that of the Warsaw Pact. When the United States is taken into consideration, the Alliance's human resources are nearly twice as large as those of the Soviet Union and Eastern Europe.[2] The means to counter the Warsaw Pact exist. The Alliance, however, needs to organize those resources in a more efficient manner in order "to get more bang for its buck"—to use the vernacular.

If the Alliance or individual European nations fail to take the lead in this area, then the United States should. Quietly but firmly within the Alliance framework, we should push our European allies to consider economies of scale and increased contributions for the common defense that result in a more favorable expenditure of funds for European defense. If this ultimately means joint production of different weapons systems, cooperative arms agreements, more standardization and eventually a more rational multinational logistical system within the NATO framework, so be it. Each member of the Alliance—the United States included— may have to compromise somewhat on its parochial views and desires to protect national defense industries, but if such initiatives would lead to enhanced defense and deterrence on the European continent, everyone would ultimately profit.

In conclusion, the policy that has guided American national security planning throughout most of the twentieth century—i.e., the desire to see that the Eurasian continent is not dominated by a power hostile to the United States—is as valid today as it was in 1917, 1939, or 1948. The strategy—forward deployment of American forces, including substantial numbers of ground forces in Western Europe that implies an acceptance of shared risks and responsibilities—appears equally valid, despite changes in the strategic environment. Before changing either the policy or strategy that has resulted in nearly a generation of stability in Europe, those who favor dramatic changes in the Alliance's doctrine, force posture, and decisionmaking structure should be required to pass the "we will be better off test." To date, they have not been able to do this. Until they can pass such a test, there should be no significant changes in U.S. policy or strategy vis-à-vis NATO.

# Notes

## Chapter 1

1. David P. Calleo, "NATO's Middle Course," *Foreign Policy*, no. 69 (Winter 1987–88), p. 142.

2. In his United Nations address, Gorbachev offered to reduce Soviet forces in Eastern Europe unilaterally by 6 tank divisions, 5,000 tanks, and 50,000 personnel and overall Soviet forces in the European portion of USSR by 10,000 tanks, 8,500 artillery systems, 800 combat aircraft, and 500,000 personnel. For detailed excerpts of Gorbachev's UN speech see the *Washington Post*, December 8, 1988, p. A32.

3. See Gregory D. Foster, "Public Opinion and the Alliance: A Strategy Framework," *Strategic Review*, vol. 15, no. 1 (Winter 1987), pp. 52–66 for a good analysis of why the United States needs to develop a public diplomacy campaign to develop Alliance consensus among European publics not just the elites.

4. For a fuller discussion of the agenda that NATO needs to confront in the future see Richard L. Kugler, "Warsaw Pact Forces and the Conventional Military Balance in Central Europe: Trends, Prospects, and Choices for NATO," *The Jerusalem Journal of International Relations*, vol. 8, nos. 2–3 (1986), pp. 15–47; and Andrew Hamilton, "Redressing the Conventional Balance: NATO's Reserve Military Manpower," *International Security*, vol. 10 no. 1 (Summer 1985), pp. 111–136.

5. North Atlantic Assembly Committee, *NATO in the 1990s* (Brussels, Belgium: North Atlantic Assembly, 1988), p. 34.

6. By "actionable" warning I mean warning of an impending conflict provided by the intelligence community that is sufficiently believable and irrefutable that political decisionmakers will be willing to act and start the NATO mobilization process. Most informed observers have few doubts that the American and Allied intelligence communities will provide political decisionmakers strategic warning of a major Warsaw Pact mobilization. The unresolved questions, as Jeffrey Simon said in his testimony before the Defense Policy Panel of the House Committee on Armed Services, are: ". . . how credible will the warning be? Will it be credible in the sense that the national political authorities will be able to go to their publics and say, 'It is now necessary for us to initiate mobilization.' This means severe social and economic dislocation. It could bring down a government." (p. 14) For more on the issue of "actionable" warning see U.S. Congress, Committee on Armed Services House of Representatives, Report of the Defense

Policy Panel, *Soviet Readiness for War: Assessing one of the Major Sources of East-West Instability*, 100th Cong., 2nd Session, 1988.

7. See for example U.S. Joint Chiefs of Staff, *United States Military Posture for FY 1980: An Overview by General David C. Jones, USAF, Chairman of the Joint Chiefs of Staff* (Washington, DC: U.S. Government Printing Office, 1979) and Andrew Marshall, "Sources of Soviet Power: The Military Potential in the 1980's," *Prospects of Soviet Power in the 1980's*, Adelphi Papers no. 152 (London: International Institute for Strategic Studies, Summer 1979).

8. Department of Defense, *Report of the Secretary of Defense, FY 1983 Budget, FY 1984 Authorization Request and FY 1983–1987 Defense Programs*, (Washington, DC: U.S. Government Printing Office, 1982), pp. I—15–16.

9. Fred Charles Ikle, "NATO's 'First Nuclear Use': A Deepening Trap?" *Strategic Review*, vol. 8, no. 1 (Winter 1980), pp. 22–23.

10. For some of the early criticisms of the Maritime Strategy see Robert W. Komer, "Maritime Strategy versus Coalition Defense," *Foreign Affairs*, vol. 60, no. 5 (Summer 1982), pp. 1124–1144; Komer, *Maritime Strategy or Coalition Defense?* (Cambridge, MA: Abt Books, 1984); Barry R. Posen, "Inadvertent Nuclear War? Escalation and NATO's Northern Flank," vol. 7, no. 2 (Fall 1982), pp. 28–54; Keith A. Dunn and William O. Staudenmaier, *Strategic Implications of the Continental-Maritime Debate* (New York: Praeger Publishers, 1984); and Dunn and Staudenmaier, "Strategy for Survival," *Foreign Policy*, no. 52 (Fall 1983), pp. 22–42.

11. Linton F. Brooks, "Conflict Termination Through Maritime Leverage," in *Conflict Termination and Military Strategy: Coercion, Persuasion, and War*, eds. Stephen J. Cimbala and Keith A. Dunn (Boulder, CO: Westview Press, 1987), pp. 161–174.

12. Stanley R. Sloan, "European Co-operation and the Future of NATO: In Search of a New Transatlantic Bargain," *Survival*, vol. 26, no. 6 (November/December 1984), p. 246.

13. Robert S. Greenberger, "Lawmakers Say They Resent Spending Billions on Defense While Allies Do Little To Contribute," *Wall Street Journal* (June 30, 1987), p. 72.

14. This is one of the arguments that Calleo has made. See Calleo, "NATO's Middle Course," pp. 135–147; and Calleo, *Beyond American Hegemony: The Future of the Western Alliance* (New York: Basic Books, Inc. Publishers, 1988).

15. See The Report of the President's Commission on Industrial Competitiveness, *Global Competition: The New Reality* (Washington, DC: U.S. Government Printing Office, 1985); and Barry P. Bosworth and Robert Z. Lawrence, "America's Global Role: From Dominance to Interdependence," in *Restructuring American Foreign Policy*, ed. John D. Steinbruner (Washington, DC: The Brookings Institution, 1988), pp. 12–47.

16. According to Stanley R. Sloan, a NATO specialist at the Congressional Research Service, "I've been working on this issue for 12 years . . ." and "in the last 12 months, I've seen more requests [for information] on burden sharing and troops abroad than in the whole previous period." Comment in David C. Morrison, "Sharing NATO's Burden," *National Journal* (May 5, 1987), p. 1394.

17. See for example, Henry A. Kissinger, *The Troubled Partnership: A Reappraisal of the Atlantic Alliance* (New York: McGraw-Hill Book Company, 1965).

18. Gregory F. Treverton, *Making the Alliance Work: The United States and Western Europe* (Ithaca, NY: Cornell University Press, 1985), p. 2.

19. Irving Kristol, "What's Wrong with NATO?" *New York Times Magazine* (September 25, 1983), p. 68; and Kristol, "Does NATO Exist?" *Washington Quarterly*, vol. 2, no. 4 (Autumn 1979), p. 45.

20. Melvyn Krauss, *How NATO Weakens the West* (New York: Simon and Schuster, 1986), p. 83.

21. Alan Ned Sabrosky, "Allies, Clients and Encumbrances," *International Security Review*, vol. 5, no. 2 (Summer 1980), p. 140.

22. For arguments along these lines see *Discriminate Deterrence*, Report of the Commission on Integrated Long-Term Strategy (Washington, DC: U.S. Government Printing Office, January 1988); and Remarks by James H. Webb, Jr., Secretary of the Navy, to the National Press Club, Washington, DC, January 13, 1988 (mimeograph). Fred C. Ikle, Under Secretary of Defense for Policy, was co-chairman of the *Discrimanate Deterrence* report. Although the Administration attempted to distance itself politically from both the report and the Webb speech, the mere fact that serving Administration officials made such comments caused many people—particularly Europeans—to wonder how much implicit official sanction for these positions in fact existed.

23. Paul Kennedy, *The Rise and Fall of the Great Powers: Economic Change and Military Conflict from 1500 to 2000* (New York: Random House, 1987), p. 432.

24. Ruth Leger Sivard, *World Social and Military Expenditures, 1987–1988* (Washington, DC: World Priorities, 1987), pp. 43–45.

25. When Franz Joseph Strauss returns from a visit to Moscow saying that the West no longer has to fear an "offensive, aggressive intention on the part of the Soviet Union," it is clear that the Soviet campaign is having an effect in Western Europe. See *The Week in Germany* (New York: German Information Center, January 8, 1988), p. 2.

# Chapter 2

1. Robert W. Komer, "Thinking About Strategy: A Practitioner's Perspective," in *Alternative Military Strategies for the Future*, eds. Keith A. Dunn and William O. Staudenmaier (Boulder, CO: Westview Press, 1985), p. viii.

2. See John Gaddis, *Strategies of Containment: A Critical Appraisal of Postwar American National Security Policy* (New York: Oxford University Press, 1982) for an excellent description of how the various postwar administrations have attempted to execute the concept of containment.

3. Christopher Layne, "Ending the Alliance," *Journal of Contemporary Studies*, vol. 6 no. 3 (Summer 1983), p. 8.

4. Samuel P. Huntington, "The Renewal of Strategy," in *The Strategic Imperative: New Policies for American Security*, ed. Samuel P. Huntington (Cambridge, MA: Ballinger Publishing Co., 1982), p. 3.

98                                                                    *Notes*

5. See for example Jeffrey Record and Robert J. Hanks, *US Strategy at the Crossroads: Two Views* (Cambridge, MA: Institute for Foreign Policy Analysis, Inc., 1982) and Zbigniew Brzezinski, *Game Plan: How to Conduct the U.S.-Soviet Contest* (Boston: The Atlantic Monthly Press, 1986).

6. See for example the arguments made by Earl C. Ravenal, "Europe Without America: The Erosion of NATO," *Foreign Affairs*, vol. 63, no. 5 (Summer 1985), pp. 1020–1035; Ravenal, "A Strategy of Restraint for the United States," in *Alternative Military Strategies for the Future*, eds. Keith A. Dunn and William O. Staudenmaier (Boulder, CO: Westview Press, 1985), pp. 177–207; David P. Calleo, "NATO's Middle Course," *Foreign Policy*, no. 69 (Winter 1987–88), pp. 135–147; Calleo, *Beyond American Hegemony: The Future of the Western Alliance* (New York: Basic Books Inc. Publishers, 1987); and Paul Kennedy *The Rise and Fall of the Great Powers: Economic Change and Military Conflict from 1500 to 2000* (New York: Random House, Inc., 1987).

7. Robert K. Komer, "Maritime Strategy versus Coalition Defense," *Foreign Affairs*, vol. 60, no. 5 (Summer 1982), pp. 1124–1144; Komer, "Is Conventional Defense of Europe Feasible?" *Naval War College Review*, vol. 35, no. 5 (September-October, 1982), pp. 80–91; and Komer, *Maritime Strategy or Coalition Defense?* (Cambridge, MA: Abt Books, 1984).

8. See arguments made by Francis Fukuyama, "Gorbachev and the Third World," *Foreign Affairs*, vol. 64, no. 4 (Spring 1986), pp. 715–731; Jerry F. Hough, *The Struggle for the Third World: Soviet Debates and American Options* (Washington, DC: The Brookings Institution, 1985); and Daniel S. Papp, *Soviet Policies Toward the Developing World During the 1980s: The Dilemmas of Power and Presence* (Maxwell Air Force Base, AL: Air University Press, 1986).

9. See Michael MccGwire, *Military Objectives in Soviet Foreign Policy* (Washington, DC: The Brookings Institution, 1987) for an excellent description of Soviet concerns about nuclear escalation and how those concerns have affected Soviet military strategy, doctrine, force development and regional allocation of its forces.

10. I would be the first to admit that rarely, if ever, do political decisionmakers express their intensity of interests in such a specific manner. Rather, decisionmakers tend to talk in vague generalities more often than not referring to everything as vital or extremely important. Obviously, too much specificity in one's declaratory policy can be counterproductive giving an adversary too clear an idea of what or what not the United States might do under a particular set of circumstances. The Korean War is a good example. Nevertheless, too much vagueness in terms of response, commitments, and intensity of interests when it confuses oneself is never a virtue. For more discussion on the pitfalls associated with not identifying one's intensity of interest and how the lack of a clear statement by political decisionmakers complicates the strategy process see Keith A. Dunn, "The Missing Link in Conflict Termination Thought: Strategy," in *Conflict Termination and Military Strategy: Coercion, Persuasion, and War*, eds. Stephen J. Cimbala and Keith A. Dunn (Boulder, CO: Westview Press, 1987), pp. 175–193.

11. I like to use this method because it is one that is accepted within the formal strategy community within the Pentagon. Another method has been used

by Donald Nuechterlein. He defines intensity of interests as survival, vital, major, and peripheral. Whether one uses Nuechterlein's paradigm or the one I propose, the important point is still the same: some statement or understanding about a nation's intensity of interest in a given area or activity is necessary in order to determine the level of risk that a nation is willing to accept to defend that interest. See Nuechterlein, *United States National Interests in a Changing World* (Lexington, KY: The University Press of Kentucky, 1973) and *American Overcommitted: United States National Interests in the 1890s* (Lexington, KY: The University Press of Kentucky, 1985).

12. MccGwire, *Military Objectives in Soviet Foreign Policy,* pp. 36–66.

13. "The extent of domination by the ground force is indicated by the fact that of the twenty military officers who are full members of the Central Committee of the Communist Party, fifteen come from the ground forces. The other four branches of service and the main political administration only rate one place each. The minor role played by the navy in the development of Soviet military thought is suggested by the relative number of service academies at the command and staff level and of book titles in the Officers' Library series. . . .

[N]aval planning, and naval procurement has been tailored to Russia's particular requirement and not to some idealized perception of what a navy should be.

What is more, the army-oriented leadership has required the navy to undertake tasks that have violated traditional assumptions about naval operations and forced the development of radical concepts. . . .

The dominance of the ground force way of thinking can be seen in the concept of close shadowing Sixth Fleet carriers with a gun-armed destroyer. The unit was acting as a forward observation post, and in the event of war would call down fire on the carriers. . . .

The idea of territorial defense, of defending 'areas' of sea and of defense in depth, rather than securing the use of the sea, also reflects a ground force way of thinking, as well as the influence of Russia's geostrategic circumstances." *Ibid.,* pp. 122–124.

14. The numbers for divisions and associated equipment used in this section and next one were derived from International Institute for Strategic Studies, *Military Balance, 1988–1989* (London: IISS, 1988): Office of the Secretary of Defense, *Soviet Military Power: An Assessment of the Threat 1988* (Washington, DC: U.S. Government Printing Office, 1988); and North Atlantic Treaty Organization, *Conventional Forces in Europe: The Facts* (Brussels, Belgium: NATO Information Service, 1988).

15. See Michael R. Gordon, "Soviets Limiting Quick-Strike Ability," *New York Times* (January 26, 1989), p. 10 and Jackson Diehl, "Two More Soviet Allies Announce Arms Cuts," *Washington Post* (January 28, 1989), p. A17.

16. The 20,000 plus tank calculation is based on Soviet and East European tanks located in the Southwestern TVD; Soviet tanks in the Northern TVD and Central Reserve; and approximately 3,000 tanks from the North Caucasus and Trans-Caucasus Military Districts that could be deployed against Turkey depending on the scenario.

17. East European divisions were left out of this calculation because it is difficult to determine if they meet standards that equate to Soviet Category I divisions.

18. Remarks by James H. Webb, Jr., Secretary of the Navy, to the National Press Club, Washington, DC, January 13, 1988 (mimeograph); and William Matthews, "Lehman: NATO Priority Shrinks," *Defense News* (September 29, 1986), p. 1.

## Chapter 3

1. John Gaddis, *Strategies of Containment: A Critical Appraisal of Postwar American National Security Policy* (New York: Oxford University Press, 1982), p. 285.

2. For arguments along these lines see Zbigniew Brzezinski, *Game Plan: How to Conduct the U.S.-Soviet Contest* (Boston: Atlantic Monthly Press, 1986); Remarks by James H. Webb, Jr., Secretary of the Navy, to the National Press Club, Washington, DC, January 13, 1988 (mimeograph); and Eliot Cohen, "Do We Still Need Europe?" *Commentary*, vol. 81, no. 1 (January 1986), pp. 28–35.

3. For a discussion of the four national interests common to all nations see Chapter 2 and particularly note 11.

4. John E. Reilly, "America's State of Mind," *Foreign Policy*, no. 66 (Spring 1987), pp. 46 and 48.

5. William Matthews, "Lehman: NATO Priority Shrinks," *Defense News* (September 29, 1986), p. 1. At the time, Secretary Lehman and the Department of the Navy argued that the reporter misquoted the Secretary.

6. Remarks by James H. Webb, Jr., Secretary of the Navy, to the National Press Club, Washington, DC, January 13, 1988 (mimeograph). For quotes see text of speech pages 3 and 11.

7. Statistics based on U.S. Department of State, Bureau of Public Affairs, *Atlas of United States Foreign Relations*, 2nd edition (Washington, DC: U.S. Government Printing Office, 1985), pp. 56–59.

8. *Ibid.*, pp. 66–67. Adding the OPEC nations—even those that do not fall within anyone's definition of Asia—would increase the Japan/Asia foreign direct investment in the United States to no more than 12 percent of the total or $20 billion.

9. Earl Ravenal and Robert Tucker have argued this point eloquently in several places. See Earl C. Ravenal, "Europe Without America: The Erosion of NATO," *Foreign Affairs*, vol. 63, no. 5 (Summer 1985), pp. 1020–1035; Ravenal, "A Strategy of Restraint for the United States," in *Alternative Military Strategies for the Future*, eds. Keith A. Dunn and William O. Staudenmaier (Boulder, Colo.: Westview Press, 1985), pp. 177–207; and Robert Tucker, "Containment and the Search for Alternatives: A Critique," in *Beyond Containment: Alternative American Policies Toward the Soviet Union*, ed. Aaron Wildavsky (San Francisco: Institute for Contemporary Studies Press, 1983), pp. 63–92.

10. Colin Gray, *Maritime Strategy, Geopolitics, and the Defense of the West* (New York: National Strategy Information Center, Inc., 1986), p. 30.

11. See Robert Tucker, "The Atlantic Alliance and Its Critics," *Commentary* (May 1982), pp. 63–72.

12. For an excellent discussion of Soviet military strategy and its evolution over the last 20 years see Michael MccGwire, *Military Objectives in Soviet Foreign Policy* (Washington, DC: The Brookings Institution, 1987).

13. For more extensive explanation of my concerns about the strategic and operational limitations associated with both land and maritime versions of horizonal escalations see Keith A. Dunn and William O. Staudenmaier, *Strategic Implications of the Continental-Maritime Debate* (New York: Praeger Publishers, 1984); Dunn and Staudenmaier, "Strategy for Survival," *Foreign Policy,* no. 52 (Fall 1983), pp. 22–42; Dunn and Staudenmaier, "The Retaliatory Offensive and Operational Realities in NATO," *Survival,* vol. 27 no. 3 (May/June 1985), pp. 108–118.

14. For a discussion of the operational and strategic problems facing the USSR in Iran specifically and Southwest Asia in general see Keith A. Dunn, "Constraints on the USSR in Southwest Asia: A Military Analysis," *ORBIS,* vol. 25, no. 3 (Fall 1981), pp. 607–630; Joshua M. Epstein, "Soviet Vulnerability in Iran and the RDF Deterrent," *International Security,* vol. 6, no. 2 (Fall 1981), pp. 126–158; Epstein, *Strategy and Force Planning: The Case of the Persian Gulf* (Washington, DC: The Brookings Institution, 1986); and Thomas L. McNaugher, *Arms and Oil: U.S. Military Strategy and the Persian Gulf* (Washington, DC: The Brookings Institution, 1985).

15. Klaus Arnhold, "The US Commitment to Europe," in *International Essays, II,* by the International Fellows of the National Defense University (Washington, DC: The National Defense University Press, 1987), p. 76.

16. Based on estimated population of 309.5 million of which 61.5 percent claim to be White and three-fourths of those claiming to be White claim European ancestral roots.

17. Studies by the Chicago Council on Foreign Relations support the contention that the American public understands the geostrategic importance of Europe to the United States. In its most recent survey, 70 percent of the general public and 85 percent of the surveyed opinion leaders believed that the United States should either keep American force levels in Europe at the current levels or increase them. When asked to choose between graduallly withdrawing U.S. forces from Europe to allow Europeans to bear a greater share of their defense burden and leaving U.S. forces in Europe, 82 percent of the opinion leaders favored leaving U.S. forces in Europe. Additionally, 63 percent of the general public and 93 percent of the leaders favored sending troops to Europe in the event of a Soviet invasion. See John E. Rielly, "America's State of Mind," *Foreign Policy,* no. 66 (Spring, 1987), pp. 46–49. See John E. Rielly, ed., *American Public Opinion and U.S. Foreign Policy 1983* (Chicago: The Chicago Council on Foreign Relations, 1983) for an earlier analysis on the same topics.

## Chapter 4

1. Zbigniew Brzezinski, *Game Plan: How to Conduct the U.S.-Soviet Contest* (Boston: Atlantic Monthly Press, 1986), p. 204.

2. Jeffrey Record and Robert Hanks, *U.S. Strategy at the Crossroads: Two Views* (Cambridge, MA: Institute for Foreign Policy Analysis, Inc., 1982), p. 5.

3. Melvyn Krauss, *How NATO Weakens the West* (New York: Simon and Schuster, 1986), p. 23.

4. In his recent book, Krauss uses Sweden to try to suggest that "welfare states" are uninterested in defense. He points out that Sweden's defense spending as a share of its gross national product dropped from over 4 percent to less than 4 percent as Sweden's rate of economic growth fell from an average of 4.4 percent in the 1960s to 1.7 percent in the 1970s. Then incomprehensibly he rejects the idea that there is or should be some cause and effect relationship between domestic economic performance and the defense spending. If that were the case, then Krauss should be equally critical of the United States in the 1970s and in the post 1987 period—which he is not—as it cut defense spending because of domestic economic considerations. Suffice it to say the argument by Krauss and others like him is ludicrous and should not receive the public attention that it has. There is a connection between overall economic performance and defense spending in democratic countries where political leaders are more often than not elected or removed from office because of their success or failure in dealing with economic issues that affect taxpayers on a day-to-day basis.

5. For example, Steven L. Canby and Ingemar Dorger have argued that if our continental allies would concentrate on providing the ground forces and reduce their investments in air and naval forces NATO could double its "present forces on the central front." To offset the reductions in European air and naval forces, the United States would move additional U.S. air force and naval assets to Europe. See Canby and Dorger, "More Troops, Fewer Missiles," *Foreign Policy*, no. 53 (Winter 1983–84), pp. 10–17.

6. Derived from International Institute for Strategic Studies, *Military Balance, 1975–1976* (London: IISS, 1975) and *Military Balance, 1987–88* (London: IISS, 1987). French, Spanish, and U.S. forces in Europe are not a part of these percentages.

7. Figures based on calculations from IISS, *Military Balance 1986–1987*, pp. 226–227. See Eurogroup, *Western Defense: The European Role in NATO* (Brussels: Eurogroup Secretariat, 1985), p. 6 for a slighter higher assessment of Europe's contribution to its own defense as expressed in terms of "outputs."

8. Maneuver damage alone in the FRG amounted to over $40 million in 1984. Real estate for NATO forces stationed in Germany, which is provided at no cost, is valued between $18–30 billion. Additionally, the West Germans endure approximately 580,000 military sorties annually of which 110,000 are low level flights (250–500 feet), including night low-level flights. See Federal Republic of Germany, Press and Information Office, *The German Contribution to the Common Defense* (Bonn, 1986), pp. 21–22 and John Galvin, "NATO After Zero INF," *Armed Forces Journal International*, vol. 125, no. 3 (March 1988), p. 58.

9. James M. Dorsey, "Allies Would Appease Soviets if U.S. Left NATO, Envoy Warns," *Washington Times* (February 19, 1987), p. 4.

10. Quoted in David C. Morrison, "Sharing NATO's Burden," *National Journal* (May 30, 1987), p. 1398.

11. Statement of Robert F. Hale, Assistant Director National Security Division, Congressional Budget Office, before the Defense Burdensharing Panel, Committee on Armed Services U.S. House of Representatives, May 10, 1988 (mimeograph), p. 5.

12. John Newhouse, ed., *U.S. Troops in Europe: Issues, Costs, and Choices* (Washington, D.C.: The Brookings Institution, 1971), p. 113–117.

13. *Ibid.,* p. 117.

14. See Department of Defense, *Report of the Secretary of Defense 1985 Authorization Request and FY 1984–1988 Defense Programs* (Washington, D.C.: U.S. Government Printing Office, 1983), pp. 186–190.

15. Congressional Budget Office, "Costs of Withdrawing Army Troops from Europe," Memorandum, May 8, 1987, p. 1. Emphasis added.

16. IISS, *Military Balance, 1983–1984,* pp. 145–149. For an excellent discussion of the impact of demographic trends on NATO countries' military capabilities see Susan Clark, *Demographics and the Military Balance: NATO in the Nineties,* IDA Paper P-2049 (Washington, DC: Institute for Defense Analysis, September 1987).

17. Telephone conversation with OSD International Security Policy (European and NATO Policy), March 23, 1988.

18. Martin Sieff, "Soviets May Lure Germany out of NATO France Warns," *Washington Times* (November 13, 1987), p. 10.

19. For an excellent German perspective on the problems and opportunities associated with enhanced Franco-German defense cooperation see Michael Sturmer, "Franco-German Defense Cooperation: Prospects, Problems, and Alternatives," in *NATO in the Fifth Decade,* eds. Keith A. Dunn and Stephen J. Flanagan, (Washington, DC: National Defense University Press, forthcoming 1989), Chapter 6.

20. Timothy P. Ireland, *Creating the Entangling Alliance: The Origins of the North Atlantic Treaty Organization* (Westport, Conn.: Greenwood Press, 1981), p. 227.

21. Josepf Joffe, "Europe's American Pacifier," *Foreign Policy,* No. 54 (Spring 1984), pp. 64–82.

22. In 1987, 70 percent of the American public and 85 percent of the opinion leaders believed that the United States should keep American forces level in Europe at current levels or increase them. John E. Rielly, "America's State of Mind," *Foreign Policy,* no. 66 (Spring, 1987), pp. 46–49.

23. James A. Thomson and Nanette C. Gantz, *Conventional Arms Control Revisited: Objectives and the New Phase,* N-2697-AF (Santa Monica: CA: RAND Corporation, 1987).

24. For example Syria has more than 4,000 T-54/55, T-62, and T-72 tanks; Libya has 2,100 T-54/55, T-62 and T-72 Tanks; and Cuba has over 1,000 T-34, T-54/55, T-62, and PT 76 tanks.

25. The 15 divisions include: the 82nd Airborne Division, 101st Air Assault, 7th Light Infantry Division, 10th Mountain Division, 25th Light Infantry Division (all of which are active), 5 Army National Guard Infantry Divisions and 1 Army National Guard Light Infantry Division, and 3 Active and 1 Reserve Marine

Divisions. I have not included the 6th Light Infantry Division in these numbers because of its U.S. continental defense mission which makes it unlikely that it would ever be used for a contingency outside of the U.S. Also, the 9th Motorized Division is not included because it will be converted to a mechanized division in the future. The 2nd Infantry Division currently is "tied" down in Korea and is not included because it is unavailable for any other contingency. Additionally, its structure is unique to any division in the U.S. inventory. While called an infantry division, it is not quite an infantry division but neither is it a mechanized division.

26. Record and Hanks, *US Strategy at the Crossroads*, pp. 28–36.

## Chapter 5

1. North Atlantic Assembly, *NATO in the 1990's* (Brussels, Belgium: North Atlantic Assembly, 1988); Leonard Sullivan, Jr., Jack A. LeCuyer, and the Atlantic Council Working Group on Comprehensive Security, *Comprehensive Security and Western Prosperity* (Lanham, MD: University Press of America, Inc., 1988); and *NATO: Meeting the Coming Challenge* (Washington, DC: The Center for Strategic and International Studies, 1988).

2. For example, in 1986, 31 percent of the West Germans said that the FRG was not militarily threatened. This was a 15 percentage point decline from 1983. See Werner Soergel, "America and the Germans," in *America and the Germans: A Study on the Behalf of the Friedrich-Ebert Stiftung and the News Magazine Stein* (Bonn, Federal Republic of Germany: Friedrich-Ebert-Stiftung, 1987), p. 43. See also Gregory Flynn and Hans Rattinger, eds., *The Public and the Atlantic Defense* (London: Croom Helm Limited, 1985), for a similar conclusion from public opinion surveys conducted in a variety of West European countries.

3. North Atlantic Treaty Organization, *Conventional Forces in Europe: The Facts* (Brussels, Belgium: NATO Information Service, 1988).

4. See *Whence the Threat to Peace?* 4th edition (Moscow: Novosti Press Agency Publishing House, 1987).

5. David M. Abshire, "Challenges to NATO in the 1990s," *Atlantic Community Quarterly*, vol. 25, no. 3 (Fall 1987), p. 281.

6. Henry Kissinger and Cyrus Vance, "Bipartisan Objectives for American Foreign Policy," *Foreign Affairs*, vol. 66, no. 5 (Summer 1988), p. 908.

7. For a discussion in support of a no first use policy see McGeorge Bundy, George F. Kennan, Robert S. McNamara and Gerald Smith, "Nuclear Weapons and the Atlantic Alliance, *Foreign Affairs*, vol. 60, no. 2 (Spring 1982), pp. 753–768; McGeorge Bundy, "'No First Use' Needs Careful Study," *Bulletin of the Atomic Scientists*, vol. 38, no. 6 (June 1982), pp. 6–8; and Robert S. McNamara, "The Military Role of Nuclear Weapons: Perceptions and Misconceptions," *Foreign Affairs*, vol. 62, no. 1 (Fall 1983), pp. 59–80.

8. John Mearsheimer, "Nuclear Weapons and Deterrence in Europe," *International Security*, vol. 9, no. 3 (Winter 1984–85), p. 22.

9. For an excellent summary of this school of thought see Stephen J. Flanagan, *NATO's Conventional Defences: Options for the Central Region* (London: Macmillan Press LTD, 1988), pp. 112–120.

10. Samuel P. Huntington, "The Renewal of Strategy," in *The Strategic Imperative: New Policies for American Security*, ed. Samuel P. Huntington (Cambridge, MA: Ballinger, 1982), pp. 21–32. LTG Richard Lawrence, USA (ret.), at the time a Major General and Commandant of the U.S. Army War College, was intrigued with Huntington's concept and asked Col. William O. Staudenmaier and myself to organize a conference that would have Huntington refine and develop his concept more fully and at the same time bring together a group of experts to explore the positive and negative politico-military factors associated with NATO adopting a conventional retaliatory strategy. For the proceedings of that conference see Dunn and Staudenmaier, eds., *Military Strategy in Transition: Defense and Deterrence in the 1990s* (Boulder, CO: Westview Press, 1984).

11. See Flanagan, *NATO's Conventional Defences*, pp. 112–120 for a good critique of the non-provocative defense concepts. See Dunn and Staudenmaier, "A NATO Conventional Retaliatory Strategy: Strategic and Force Structure Implications," in *Military Strategy in Transition*, pp. 187–212; and Dunn and Staudenmaier, "The Retaliatory Offensive and Operational Realities in NATO," *Survival*, vol. 27, no. 3 (May/June 1985), pp. 108–118 for critiques of Huntington's proposals.

12. Huntington claimed that the intent of his proposal was not to change NATO doctrine and strategy but rather to "make flexible response more flexible and forward defense more forward . . .

A broad consensus already exists on the need to enhance conventional deterrence. The political support of NATO governments and peoples for moving in this direction will in due course emerge, as is true of any new policy, from consideration of the unpalatability of the alternative." Huntington, "Conventional Deterrence and Conventional Retaliation in Europe," in *Military Strategy in Transition*, p. 37.

13. In our critique, William Staudenmaier and I calculated that NATO would require an additional 20 U.S. and 11 NATO divisions to successfully execute a conventional retaliatory strategy as outlined by Huntington. Even if our calculations were off by a factor of two the financial cost alone for the United States would have been more than $80 million over a five year period to create ten new divisions. Such expenditures were not possible in 1985 and are even more unlikely now given budget realities. See Dunn and Staudenmaier, "The Retaliatory Offensive and Operational Realities in NATO," in *Military Strategy in Transition*, pp. 112 and 114.

14. The five key mission areas were: (1) defeating forward deployed Warsaw Pact forces; (2) neutralizing Warsaw Pact reinforcing formations; (3) obtaining a favorable NATO air environment; (4) protecting rear areas; and (5) controlling the maritime approaches to the European continent. Michael Reynolds, Michael Vollstedt, and Malcolm Hunt, "The Conceptual Military Framework," *NATO's Sixteen Nations* (December 1985), pp. 31–35.

15. *Ibid.* p. 35.

16. Christopher Donnelly, "The Soviet Operational Manoeuvre Group: A New Challenge for NATO," *International Defense Review*, vol. 15, no. 9 (September 1982), pp. 1177–1186; John G. Hines and Phillip A. Petersen, "The Soviet

Conventional Offensive in Europe," *Military Review,* vol. 64, no. 4 (April 1984), pp. 3–29; and David Greenwood, "Strengthening Conventional Deterrence: Doctrine, New Technology and Resources," *NATO Review,* vol. 32, no. 4 (August 1984), pp. 8–11.

17. Andrew Hamilton, "Redressing the Conventional Balance: NATO's Reserve Military Manpower," *International Security,* vol. 10, no. 1 (Summer 1985), pp. 127–131.

18. Karl E. Lowe, "Enhancing NATO's Conventional Defenses," unpublished paper, May 10, 1988.

19. See Jeffrey Simon, ed., *NATO-Warsaw Pact Force Mobilization* (Washington, DC: National Defense University Press, 1988) for an indepth discussion of the potential civilian assets available to West European nations that are not formally considered in the NATO planning process because they fall under national authority.

20. For a good discussion of the French policy of "no automaticity" see David S. Yost, *France and Conventional Defense in Central Europe,* (Boulder, CO: Westview Press, 1985), pp. 13–20.

21. For an excellent discussion of NATO port facilities and capabilities see F.A. L. Alstead, *Ten in Ten?: A Study of the Central Region Transport Capability in Crisis and War* (Brussels: North Atlantic Treaty Organization, 1988), pp 237–328.

22. *Ibid.,* p. 331. France carried its desire to remain independent to such a point that it denied permission to Brigadier General Alstead to even discuss his study with military and civilian planners in Paris.

23. Yost, *France and Conventional Defence in Central Europe,* p. 76.

24. *Ibid.;* Flanagan, *NATO's Conventional Defences,* p. 55; and Alstead, *Ten in Ten?* pp. 331–332.

25. Walter Lippman, *U.S. Foreign Policy: Shield of the Republic* (Boston: Little, Brown and Company, 1943), p. 138.

## Chapter 6

1. Robert W. Komer, *Maritime Strategy or Coalition Defense?* (Cambridge, MA: Abt Books, 1984), p. 86.

2. United States Department of State, Bureau of Public Affairs, *Atlas of United States Foreign Policy,* 2nd edition (Washington, DC: U.S. Government Printing Office, 1985), p. 40.

# About the Author

Keith A. Dunn is a senior fellow in the Institute for National Strategic Studies, National Defense University, Washington, D.C. Dr. Dunn received his Ph.D. in diplomatic history from the University of Missouri–Columbia in 1973. Subsequently he was an intelligence officer in the U.S. Army and a research analyst at the Strategic Studies Institute (SSI) of the U.S. Army War College. From 1983 to 1985 he was the senior policy analyst at SSI.

He has published widely on U.S. national security affairs, Soviet strategy and defense policy, and regional security issues. He is the author or coeditor of five other books: *Strategic Implications of the Continental-Maritime Debate* (1984); *Military Strategy in Transition: Defense and Deterrence in the 1980s* (Westview, 1985); *Alternative Military Strategies for the Future* (Westview, 1985); *Conflict Termination and Military Strategy: Coercion, Persuasion, and War* (Westview, 1987); and *NATO in the Fifth Decade* (forthcoming). Also, he is the author of sixteen major government studies and more than thirty scholarly articles.

# Index

current deployments, 34–35
exits to world, 47
geostrategic position of, 7, 20, 99(n13)
ground forces, 99(n13)
Group of Soviet Forces Germany, 36
Iran invasion, 48–49
limitations on power of, 22, 23–24
military capabilities of, 22, 32–33, 34–35, 38–39
and multi-front war, 48
naval forces, 34–35, 38–39, 43, 99(n13)
Operational Maneuver Groups (OMGs), 84, 85
perceptions of, 23
regional priorities of, 33
reinforcement capabilities of, 72
and Southwest Asia, 33
theater of military operations (TVDs) forces, 34–35
and Third World, 12, 22, 25, 48
as threat to Western Europe, 2, 23, 39
World War II strategy of, 12–13
*See also* United States, and Soviet Union
Staudenmaier, William O., 105(n10)
*Strategic Review*, 13
Strategy issues, 81–84
conventional retaliation vs. non-provocative defense, 81–83, 105(n10, 13)
and economic costs, 19–20
and global center of gravity, 24
military vs. national, 20
national strategy reviews, 90
and policy, 19–21, 41, 77, 90
strategic environment, 22–27, 38
strategic lift, 75
Strauss, Franz Joseph, 97(n25)
Suez crisis, 14
Supreme Allied Commander in Europe (SACEUR), 6, 83

Supreme Headquarters Allied Powers Europe (SHAPE), 84
Sweden, 34, 102(n4)
Syria, 24, 74, 103(n24)

Tanks, 103(n24)
Warsaw Pact, 34, 35, 36–37, 72, 95(n2), 99(n16)
Western European, 59
Territorial/home defense forces, 86–87
Third World, 24, 31
conflicts in, 2, 74, 75, 92
GNP, 45(table)
and Soviet Union, 12, 22, 25, 48
Trade issues, 4, 15, 43–44, 44(table), 53, 92
Treverton, Gregory, 15
Tucker, Robert, 47
Turkey, 48–49, 69, 71, 93
TVDs. *See* Soviet Union, theater of military operations forces

United Kingdom. *See* Great Britain
United States
alliance system of, 23, 26, 47
ancestry in, 51–52(tables)
Army, 83
basic policy of, 20, 21, 94
defense spending, 4, 20, 57, 58(fig.), 59, 102(n4)
deficits, 4, 15
demographics, 51–52, 53(table)
Department of Defense. *See* Department of Defense
development assistance of, 46–47
exports/imports, 44(table)
foreign-born persons in, 50(table)
foreign investments in, 100(n8)
foreign investments of, 45
gross domestic product, 61
immigrants in, 50
isolationism of, 72
and Israel, 30
maritime strategy, 3, 14
military force structure, 74–75

1714